Corazon Aquino
Leader of the Philippines

James Haskins

ENSLOW PUBLISHERS, INC.

Bloy St. & Ramsey Ave.   P.O. Box 38
Box 777   Aldershot
Hillside, N.J. 07205   Hants GU12 6BP
U.S.A.   U.K.

Acknowledgments

I am grateful to Ms. Marisse Reyes, Corresponding Secretary to President Aquino, to the Philippine Ministry of Tourism, and to Mrs. Genie Advincula of the Library of the Cultural Office of the Philippine Consulate for their help. Thanks also are due to Ann Jefferies for her research assistance. And a special thank-you goes to Kathy Benson.

Library of Congress Cataloging in Publication Data

Haskins. James, 1941-
  Corazon Aquino : leader of the Philippines.

  Bibliography: p.
  Includes index.
  Summary: Traces the life of the woman who won
election as the first woman president of the
Philippines in 1986.
    1. Aquino, Corazon Cojuangco—Juvenile literature.
  2. Philippines—Presidents—Biography—Juvenile
literature. [1. Aquino, Corazon Cojuangco.
  2. Philippines—Presidents] I . Title.
  DS686.616.A65H37   1988   959.9'046'0924   [B]   87-24440
  ISBN 0-89490-152-4   [92]

Printed in the United States of America

10 9 8 7 6 5 4 3 2

Illustration Credits

A/P Wide World Photos, pp. 35, 41, 47, 51, 58, 63, 65, 75, 78, 81, 85, 91, 95, 99, 109, 113, 117, 122; Courtesy of the College of Mount St. Vincent, pp. 24, 109; Courtesy of the Philippine Ministry of Tourism, p. 6; Courtesy of President Corazon Aquino, p. 18.

to Annie

Sources Used for This Book

For background on the history of the Philippines and its people, I used the three volumes of *The Filipino Nation: A Concise History of the Philippines* (Grolier International, 1982) by Helen R. Tubangui, Leslie E. Bauzon, Marcelino A. Foronda, Jr., and Luz U. Ausejo, for which I served as general editor. I also used *The Land and Peoples of the Philippines* by John Nance (J. B. Lippincott, 1977) and *The New Philippines* by Don Lawson (Franklin Watts, 1986).

For information on Cory Aquino's life and career I used a fine article by Betty Go Belmonte titled "President Cory's Early Years," which appeared in the *Fookien Times Philippines Yearbook 1985–1986,* an article by Gail Sheehy called "The Passage of Corazon Aquino" (*Parade*, June 9, 1986), an excellent two-part article in *The New Yorker* (August 25 and September 1, 1986) titled "From Aquino to Marcos" by Robert Shaplen, and articles in the *Time* magazine issue of January 5, 1987, whose cover proclaimed Cory Aquino "Woman of the Year."

For day-by-day accounts of events in the Philippines and Cory's campaign and presidency, I used *The New York Times, Time, Newsweek, U.S. News & World Report,* and other newspapers and magazines. Especially valuable were *Keesing's Contemporary Archives* (published in the United Kingdom by Longman), a record of national and international affairs based on information from press, broadcast, official, and other sources, which I consulted for the years 1972–1985.

—J.H.

Contents

I

Woman of the Year

When *Time* magazine names its Man of the Year, people around the world pay attention. *Time* is a very important news magazine, and the people it chooses are people who are making a difference in the world. But when *Time* named its Man of the Year for 1986, people really sat up and took notice. The Man of the Year was a woman!

Corazon Aquino was only the third woman to be selected since the magazine started naming a Man of the Year in 1927. In 1936 an American woman, Wallis Simpson, was the first. That year the king of England stepped down from his throne rather than give her up (she had been divorced twice, and so the British would not accept her as the king's wife). In 1952 the British Queen Elizabeth became the second Woman of the Year on the cover of *Time*. Thirty-four years later, the magazine selected another woman, and few people disagreed with its choice.

At fifty-two, "Cory" Aquino had never before held public office. Yet she toppled one of the most powerful presidents in the world and won election as the first woman president of the

Philippines. She came to power not by force but by faith, hope, and the ability to inspire a whole range of Filipino people. And she promised that she would not use her power for herself. All she wanted to do was to help the Filipino people and bring democracy to her country. She did not plan to run for election as president again.

There have been other women leaders of nations. There still are. But none of them is like Corazon Aquino. She is a first in many ways, especially in the Philippines, which does not have a tradition of female leadership.

Only once before in the history of the Philippines did a woman take up leadership of a revolution after her husband was killed. Back in the 1700s, when the Philippines was a Spanish colony, Diego Silang was the leader of a group of rebels fighting for Philippine independence. Silang was assassinated by an agent of the Spanish colonial government. His wife, Gabriela, continued the fight. Riding on horseback and wielding a bolo (a large curved knife), she was a brave fighter. But she was caught and executed.

More than two hundred years later, after her husband, Benigno Aquino, was assassinated, Corazon Aquino led a different kind of fight. She took power in the midst of a people's revolution that shed flower petals rather than blood. After becoming president, she was generous with her enemies and willing to try to work out the differences between them. She said she would rather be a grandmother than a president, but she believed that she had a mission to bring democracy to the Philippines. She felt, too, that she had a responsibility to carry on the work of her husband, who had been killed when he tried to bring democracy to their country. And she believed that God was behind her every step of the way.

When she challenged Philippine President Marcos in early 1986, most people around the world and in her own country did not believe that Cory Aquino could beat him. Once she had beaten him, most people around the world and in her own country did not believe that Cory Aquino could be a real leader. She proved these doubters wrong. She may have been a "plain housewife," but she was smart. She was a quiet woman, but she had ideas. She had grown up privileged and well educated, but she understood the poverty and despair of the majority of the Filipino people. She was a deeply religious woman, but her trust in God did not keep her from acting. In fact, it gave her the strength to act. Looking back, Cory Aquino could see that in some ways her whole life had prepared her to do just what she was doing, to be just what she was.

2

Young Cory

Maria Corazon Cojuangco was born on January 25, 1933, in Tarlac Province in the town of Paniqui, a busy railroad center about forty miles north of Manila, capital of the Philippines. From the beginning, her family called her by her middle name, *Corazon*, which means "heart" in Spanish. They shortened it to *Core* (pronounced "Co-ray"), but Americans are used to seeing it spelled *Cory*, so that is how it is spelled here.

Cory's heritage is mixed Chinese and Spanish. Her great-great-grandfather came to the Philippines from China. If *Cojuangco* doesn't sound very Chinese, that is because the family took a Spanish last name in the 1800s. The Spanish, who ruled the Philippines from the late 1500s to the late 1800s, decreed that all Filipinos must change their last names to Spanish ones. The Spanish also gave the Philippines its name. The Spaniards who reached the islands in 1543 named them in honor of Prince Felipe, son of King Charles, who later succeeded his father to the throne and ruled Spain as King Philip II.

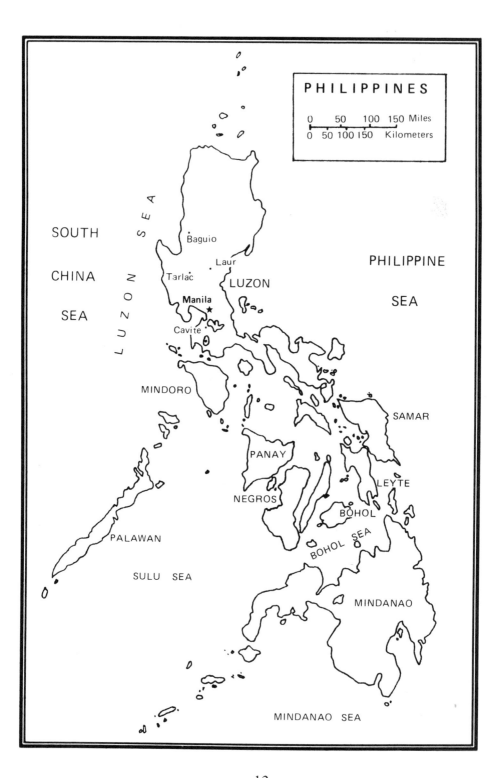

12

The Cojuangco family also converted to Catholicism once they had established themselves in the Philippines. The Spanish brought Catholicism to the islands, and the majority of Filipinos adopted that religion, making the Philippines the only area of Asia where Christianity is the main faith.

The Cojuangco family fit in and prospered. Cory's great-great-grandfather built a small rice mill and a sugar mill. His sons bought up land. Cory's parents, José and Demetria Cojuangco, were wealthy landowners. So were the other Cojuangcos, and since they all had lots of children (there were eight children in Cory's family), they quickly spread their influence in the province.

But they were a very small proportion of the Filipino population. Most Filipinos, unlike the Cojuangcos, were poor. Tarlac was only one of the many provinces on only one island in the group of more than seven thousand Pacific islands that make up the Philippines.

While the Cojuangcos were Catholic, like the majority of Filipinos, there were many Filipinos who were Moslem. Two centuries before the Spanish conquered the Philippines, the Moslem religion had spread to the area from Malaysia. In fact, it would probably have become the major religion if the Spanish had not come. After the Spanish forced the Moslems out of Manila, they moved to the southern islands of the Philippine island group, and they remained strong there even four centuries later, when Maria Corazon Cojuangco was born. They resisted all outside influences and fought bitterly for their independent way of life.

When Corazon Cojuangco was born in 1933, the Philippine islands were under the control of the United States. In 1898 the United States had captured the Philippines from the ‹Spanish, and the Filipinos had adopted many aspects of

American culture, including the English language. The Philippines became the third most populous English-speaking country in the world. But in the Philippines there remained many different languages, reflecting the various cultures that existed there—Malay and Moslem, Spanish and Chinese, not to mention the culture of the original islanders. In the late 1930s, Pilipino, a language based on Tagalog (of the eight native languages spoken in the Philippines, Tagalog was spoken by the most people), was declared the official national language. The *h* was taken out of the word *Philipino* because the people didn't want their language as well as their country to be named after a Spanish ruler. But less than half the population used Pilipino as their main language, and English continued to be used widely in government, business, the press, and higher education.

Filipinos are the result of their varied heritage. Most look Asian, are practicing Christians, and speak colloquial (everyday) English with a Spanish accent. The willingness of Filipinos to adopt the culture of the Philippines' various conquerors has caused some people to say that the islands do not have a soul. But one Filipino writer was more gentle in his criticism of his country's lack of identity. He explained that each time some other nation conquered his country, the Filipino decided that in order to survive he had to "put on the mask of the foreigner." The Filipino did manage to survive that way, "but when the time came for taking off the mask, it had become part of his face."

Nevertheless, over the years there had been strong independence movements. One of the earliest was mentioned in the first chapter—the revolution led by Diego Silang, and then later by his wife Gabriela, against the Spanish in the 1700s. One of the most famous took place in 1872 when a group of Filipino soldiers serving in the Spanish military mutinied in Cavite Province, south of Manila. The Spanish quickly put down the revolt, but they used it as an excuse for a general crackdown against people who enjoyed the loyalty and trust of the Filipinos. They arrested a number of so-called conspirators, including three priests, accused them of planning to overthrow the government, and executed them in a public square. This action only increased unrest among the people.

Twenty years later a group of men led by Andres Bonifacio formed a secret society called the Katipunan to unite the Filipinos against Spain. After only four years they had thousands of members and called publicly for revolution against Spain. Fighting broke out in several provinces, but it was concentrated in Cavite, the same province where the Filipino soldiers had mutinied in 1872.

In 1897, Emilio Aguinaldo, one of the leaders of the Katipunan, proclaimed an independent Republic of the Philippines. Since Spain was also fighting a rebellion in Cuba, the Spanish were willing to negotiate a peace treaty with the Katipunan. Unfortunately, by the time that treaty was signed, the United States had become involved in the trouble in Cuba. U.S. companies had investments in Cuba, and the battleship *Maine* was sent to Havana to protect U.S. property and citizens. The *Maine* exploded mysteriously, and the United States declared war on Spain, seeking to take over not just Cuba but the Philippines as well.

Aguinaldo did not want to exchange one foreign ruler for another. On June 12, 1898, at Kawit, Cavite, he proclaimed Philippine independence yet again. This time, he and other leaders drew up a constitution. He formally approved it on January 21, 1899, and the next day established, again, the Republic of the Philippines.

But the United States had other ideas. The U.S. Congress voted to annex the Philippines as U.S. territory, and U.S. troops went after Aguinaldo and his forces. Eventually the Philippine republic collapsed.

The United States ruled the Philippines less harshly than had Spain, allowing Filipinos a considerable say in their own affairs. The North Americans introduced free public education and better health care. They also improved the Philippine economy through trade. But many Filipinos believed that the only way the Philippines could have a soul was for the country to govern itself and to have pride in its own heritage, language, and culture.

By the time Cory was born, another independence movement was gathering strength. Many people in the United States agreed that the Philippines should be independent. The problem was that Philippine ties to the United States were very strong. In fact, the Philippine economy depended almost entirely on the United States. One year after Cory was born, U.S. President Franklin D. Roosevelt proposed a plan for gradual Philippine independence: Filipinos would write a constitution for their new nation, and ten years after the American president approved it, they would be given their independence. In the ten years between, they would be a commonwealth, under the supervision of the United States.

The new Philippine Constitution was approved in 1936, and the date for Philippine independence was set for July 4, 1946 (July 4 was chosen because that was date when the thirteen original colonies of the United States had declared their independence from Britain in 1776). None of this meant much to young Cory, who was just three years old when the Philippines became a commonwealth of the United States.

Cory was the sixth of eight children born to José and Demetria Cojuangco. The first, a son, died at birth. The second was also a son, named Pedro. Then there were Josephine and

Teresita (Terry). A third daughter, Carmen, died after she fell from her crib and hit her head. Then came Cory, José Jr. (Peping), and Maria Paz (Passy).

They lived a very comfortable life. The year Cory was born they moved to a large house on Agno Street in the Malate section of Manila. The older children were ready for school, and the Cojuangcos wanted to be near good ones in the city. They had servants, but the children were not spoiled—at least not by their mother. Cory remembers that her father was very easygoing (she calls him a "saint"). Her mother was the strict one. They were encouraged to learn to take care of themselves. They were also taught to understand the value of money and never to spend it just because it was there. As a young girl, Cory learned to sew and make her own clothing rather than go out and buy expensive dresses. At school, she wore uniforms handed down by her older sisters.

Cory started school at nearby St. Scholastica, where she was known as quiet, kind, and soft-spoken. She was also very bright. Her parents taught all their children the Latin motto *Ora et labora*—"Pray and work." Cory took that motto very seriously. She was at the top of her class every year in grade school except 1941, when her friend Angelita took that honor. Cory never boasted about her high marks. In fact, her clearest grade school memory is of the year she graduated at the top of the class because the girl with the highest grades had moved away.

Cory's best subjects were math and English. Her worst was piano. The biggest outburst she ever made at home was to cry, "I'm never going to learn [to play] the piano well!" Cory was used to doing things well, so it bothered her when she found something difficult.

Except for her troubles with the piano, Cory's early years were happy ones. At school she worked hard, but she had fun

Cory Aquino as a second grader at St. Scholastica school in Manila

as well. Once a year the nuns took the girls for an outing to the beaches in Las Pinas. Throughout the year, there were birthday parties, to which only girls were invited.

At home, the Cojuangco children sometimes went to the movies with their parents or with one of their aunts. On rare occasions, they were taken to the main street in town, Dewey Boulevard, for ice cream. The elder Cojuangcos were more interested in working than in playing, but they allowed their children to play games and to have fun. They wanted them to grow up to be well-rounded citizens who would contribute to their society and make their parents proud. Young Cory intended to live up to her parents' expectations.

3

War and Politics

In 1941, when Cory was eight, World War II came to the Pacific. Japan first attacked the U.S. naval fleet in Pearl Harbor, Hawaii, and a few hours later did the same thing in the Philippines. The United States did not have enough forces in the Philippines to put up a proper fight, and within three weeks, the capital city of Manila was abandoned to the Japanese.

The Japanese takeover did not drastically change the lives of most Filipinos. The Cojuangcos remained where they were, and the children stayed in school. The Japanese tried to form a government with the Filipinos, and while some Filipino leaders resisted them, others agreed to cooperate. Among the commonwealth officials who agreed to form a new government under the Japanese were José Laurel, minister of justice, and Benigno S. Aquino, minister of the interior. A new constitution was approved in 1943, and Laurel and Aquino were elected president and second vice-president of the new National Assembly. With the backing of the Japanese, the National Assembly then proclaimed a second Republic of the

Philippines and elected Laurel its president and Aquino Speaker of the Assembly. Cory's father, José, became a congressman. An uncle was also a congressman, and another uncle was a senator.

Both Laurel and Aquino came from wealthy families in the province of Tarlac. The Laurels, Aquinos, and Cojuangcos all knew each other, and so did their children. Cory believes that she first met her future husband, Benigno Aquino's son, Benigno Jr., who was called "Ninoy," at a birthday party for the elder Aquino. They were both nine years old. Cory was once asked if it was "love at first sight." She answered, "Heavens, no. I was nine years old. What does a nine-year-old girl feel about a nine-year-old boy? I remember Ninoy kept bragging he was a year ahead of me in school; so I didn't even bother to talk to him."

There were a lot of parties now that Cory's father was a congressman, and many powerful and important people visited the Cojuangco home. At a young age, Cory learned how to act around such people and not to be awed by them.

Meanwhile, the United States mounted a campaign to win back the Philippines. Battles raged across the islands as the tide gradually turned in favor of the United States. The capital, Manila, was heavily affected, and Cory and her schoolmates had to study between air raids. Eventually, the bombings got so bad that the Cojuangcos kept their children home from school.

But even home was not safe. The Cojuangco home in Malate was burned to the ground, and the family sought shelter in the home of their grandparents in nearby Sampaloc. Cory's uncle Antonio got word to his brother that they would be safer on the De La Salle side of the city, but the bridges were blown up, and José Cojuangco could not find transportation for his family.

As U.S. forces moved north and Japanese troops moved south, many Filipinos caught in the middle did not survive. All but two in the family of Antonio Cojuangco were massacred by the Japanese.

By early 1945 the United States were bombarding Manila, the last stronghold of the Japanese. The Japanese commander in chief ordered President José Laurel and his family to Japan. Benigno S. Aquino accompanied Laurel to Tokyo. On February 3 the Japanese finally surrendered. Two days later, President Laurel proclaimed the end of the second Philippine Republic, and that same afternoon an American colonel picked up Laurel, his son, José Laurel, Jr., and Benigno S. Aquino and took them to a Japanese prison. They remained imprisoned in Japan for nearly a year before they were returned to the Philippines. The rest of Laurel's family was sent back to the Philippines immediately, and there the Aquino and Laurel families drew even closer together in their shared sadness over the imprisonment of their men. Salvador Laurel and Benigno S. Aquino, Jr., who was five years younger, became especially close, despite the difference in their ages.

Once the United States regained control of the Philippines, it lived up to its earlier promise. As scheduled, on July 4, 1946, the Philippines was declared an independent republic. Unfortunately, it was an independent republic that had been ravaged by war. Manila was in ruins, and so was the country's economy. The war had spawned all sorts of guerrilla movements, and rebels were everywhere in the islands. One of these rebel groups had started before the war when poor landless peasants organized to fight against wealthy landowners. They were strongly influenced by the ideas of economic equality in communism and socialism. During the war, they resisted the Japanese invaders and took the name *Hukbalahap* ("People's Army Against Japan"). Called the

Huks, they were a well-armed and powerful group that did not want the Philippines to have the same kind of economic inequality that the United States had. They threatened to make trouble for the new government. Cory Cojuangco's parents did not feel that they were safe in their native country, and so in 1946 they moved to the United States to wait for the situation in the Philippines to settle down.

At age thirteen, Cory traveled with her family to the United States and settled first in Philadelphia, Pennsylvania, where she enrolled at the Raven Hill Academy, a small Catholic girls' school. After about a year the elder Cojuangcos returned to Manila, but the children stayed behind to finish their schooling. They moved to New York City to live with their mother's sister, Tita Belen.

Cory completed her junior and senior years of high school at the Notre Dame School for Girls, another small Catholic school on the Upper West Side of Manhattan. She graduated from Notre Dame in 1949 with the highest grades in her class of fourteen.

For college, Cory joined her sister Terry, two years older, at the College of Mount St. Vincent in the Bronx, also a Catholic girls' school. She and Terry and two other girls, the Fabella sisters, were the only Filipinos in a student body of 106. Cory majored in French and mathematics. Her classmates remember her as a very quiet young woman who sometimes entertained them with a Philippine dance called the Tinikling, which was performed by hopping over bamboo sticks. She once played an angel in a school play. Mostly, though, she kept to herself. She and her sister were very close. They spent weekends learning to cook at their aunt's house.

Each summer, Terry and Cory returned to the Philippines to join their family at their summer home in Baguio, in the northern part of the island of Luzon. During the summer she was seventeen, Cory met Ninoy Aquino again. He was attending Ateneo de Manila University and, at seventeen, was the youngest correspondent in history for the *Manila Times.* "There were so many parties and we kept running into each other," Cory later recalled.

Cory was not looking for a boyfriend at the time, and even if she had been, she would not have seriously considered Ninoy Aquino. He was too close to her own age. She planned to marry a man who was at least five years older than she. Her father was five years older than her mother, and anyway, at school she had learned that girls mature faster than boys. But Ninoy Aquino was different from most of the seventeen-year-old boys she knew. In fact, she later described him as "the most articulate guy I had met."

After Cory returned to New York in the fall, she and Ninoy wrote to each other often. "His love letters impressed me," she said later. "They were not mushy, for one thing."

When she graduated from the College of Mount St. Vincent in 1953, Cory was again at the head of her class. After that, she returned to the Philippines.

By this time, her native country had been rebuilt and was enjoying a period of prosperity. In return for allowing naval bases in the Philippines, the United States had been giving a great deal of aid to the war-torn country. Some Filipinos were against this U.S. aid, and the Huks and other guerrilla groups throughout the islands continued to fight against the Filipinos who were in power. The government was still unsettled for several years after the Japanese were defeated, but by 1953, when Cory graduated from college, Ramón Magsaysay had won election as president of the Philippines. His election ushered in a new period of calm in the country.

Corazon Cojuangco, age 20, in her 1953 College of Mount St. Vincent yearbook photo.

Back home, Cory enrolled in the law school at Far Eastern University in Manila. Her family had decided that it was time for the young female Cojuangcos to take an active part in the family businesses, and Cory, who'd had an excellent school record, was a prime candidate. Cory was eager herself to have a career, and she was determined to put off marriage until she had completed her degree. Besides, she explained to Ninoy that she did not feel they knew each other well enough to rush into marriage.

Ninoy, meanwhile, was already a rising star in Philippine politics. While working as a war correspondent for the *Manila Times*, he had become friends with President Magsaysay. When Magsaysay decided that he wanted the leader of the Huks, Luis Taruc, to surrender, he sent the young Benigno Aquino to talk Taruc into it. Aquino negotiated with Taruc for a long time, but finally he managed to persuade Taruc to give himself up. With Taruc's surrender, the Huks lost their most important leader and their unity. The Philippines became the first Asian country to put down a serious Communist threat, and President Magsaysay had the young Benigno Aquino to thank for it.

Ninoy was making plans for a political career and wanted Cory by his side as he climbed the political ladder. Cory wanted to get a law degree. He tried to argue her out of that. "If you're such a brain, why couldn't you have gone to better schools in the United States?" he wanted to know. Cory answered, "Maybe they weren't such classy schools, but the underlying values those nuns give you can really help you in life."

They continued to date, always accompanied by a chaperon, usually Cory's younger sister Passy. But Cory refused even to tell her parents that she and Ninoy were talking about

25

marriage. Then, in the early fall of 1954, an automobile accident forced the hand of the young couple.

Ninoy took Cory to the movies, chaperoned this time by her older sister Josephine. As they drove home in Ninoy's convertible, a jeep hit them from behind, and both Josephine and Cory were thrown out of the car. Cory was so bruised that she had to spend the night in the hospital. Her parents were very upset, and they forbade her ever to ride in Ninoy's car again. Cory recalled that when Ninoy heard that, he was quiet "for once in his life."

Cory decided it was time to tell her parents that she and Ninoy wanted to get married. Ninoy, in turn, told his. Both sets of parents approved of the match, for Cory and Ninoy came from similar backgrounds. Both their families were well-to-do and came from the province of Tarlac, and both believed that young women should be independent thinkers and not just dutiful wives. Ninoy's mother worried that her son might be a bit too independent and too quick to act without thinking. When Cory's father told her, "You'll have to be patient with Cory—she has a mind of her own," Mrs. Aquino decided that Cory might be just the right wife for her son. Perhaps Cory could calm him down a bit.

Cory's parents not only gave their immediate consent. They also suggested that the young couple get married on the anniversary of their own wedding, October 11, 1954. Although that was just ten days away, the young couple made plans in a rush and did get married on that date.

It was a morning wedding at Our Lady of the Sorrows Church in the Pasay City section of Manila, and it was attended not only by relatives and friends of both families but also by President Ramón Magsaysay. They had a wedding breakfast at the Manila Hotel, then took off for a honeymoon in the United States.

Cory hoped to continue her studies after her marriage, but Ninoy had other ideas. Almost immediately, they moved to a piece of land he had bought in the town of Concepcion in Tarlac, their native province. The province was a stronghold of Communist rebels, but Ninoy decided that it was the most likely province for his first political race. While Cory made a home and waited for the birth of their first child, Ninoy campaigned against the powerful politicians of Tarlac. He was confident that he could beat them, for he was a special friend of President Magsaysay, and President Magsaysay was a special friend of the poor people of the Philippines. When Ninoy won election as mayor of Concepcion, he became the youngest mayor in Philippine history.

President Magsaysay was the first president of the country to pay real attention to the farmers and the other landless people. He opened the presidential palace in Manila to them. He encouraged them to vote. He started a program that would give public lands to those who were landless. While he remained friendly to the United States, which the Communists did not like, he started so many programs aimed at economic equality that the Communists did not have many issues over which they could fight him. His critics said that he still hadn't given the Philippines a soul, but his supporters said that he had done more to give a soul to the Philippines than any previous president. Benigno Aquino supported him and hoped to be elected to office to work with him. Then Magsaysay's career and life were cut short. On March 17, 1957, he was killed in an airplane crash.

The Philippine Constitution, like the U.S. Constitution, provided for an orderly succession in the event of the sudden death of a president. Magsaysay's vice-president, Carlos P. Garcià, became president. New elections were scheduled to be held in eight months, and Garcia immediately launched a campaign to be elected president on his own. But Garcia did not have the unquestioned support of the farmers that Magsaysay had enjoyed. It was quite possible that a rival candidate would win the presidency.

What was certain was that Benigno Aquino could not look forward to the easy political rise that he had once expected. But he spent very little time worrying about the loss of his political friend. He simply devoted his time to making new ones and keeping the ones he still had.

In the next national elections, Garcia ran with José P. Laurel on the Nacionalista party ticket. Aquino supported them. He was still very close to the Laurel family. He and Salvador Laurel were best friends, as they had been since childhood. In fact, Ninoy would be godfather to Laurel's children. In the election, Garcia won, but Laurel lost to the Liberal party's vice-presidential candidate, Diosdado Macapagal. It was the first time in the history of Philippine politics that the top two national offices went to members of opposing parties. Benigno Aquino managed to keep ties with both those parties and with the people of Tarlac Province. By 1961 he was governor of the province—the youngest governor in the country.

The Aquino home was as busy as a hive of bees. People called and visited at all hours of the day and night. Cory was always the dutiful wife, serving coffee and snacks to her husband's visitors. They didn't pay much attention to her, but she always listened to what they were saying. Later, after they had gone, she would tell her husband what she thought about the various political situations that had been discussed. She never spoke up when other people were around, however.

"My husband, well, he was a male chauvinist," Cory told the writer Gail Sheehy. "He never wanted it said that I was influencing him in anything. I didn't mind, really, because mine was a very private role. And I figured, 'Look, *you* can do your thing in public life; *I'm* going to make sure that these children of ours will turn out to be good and responsible citizens.' And so we managed very well. If you think your husband is really worthwhile, then you just have to accept."

So Cory cared for their one son, Benigno III, and their four daughters, Viel, Maria Elena, Victoria, and Kristina, and ran the household and went to church and supported her husband. Ninoy always seemed too busy to pay much attention to her or the children, and that bothered her sometimes. But she believed in him, and she believed that if he could only achieve power in the Philippines he would do much good for the country. "Someday it will all be worth it," she told herself.

4

Troubled Waters

In the same 1961 election that made Benigno Aquino the youngest governor of a Philippine province, Vice-President Diosdado Macapagal ran against President Garcia and won. Other national and local offices changed hands as well, and in general the campaigns were extremely vicious. In some rural areas, local contests for office resulted in the deaths of several persons. There was great unrest in the country, mostly because the economy was so poor.

The problems that the Philippines had faced after the war were still there and had even worsened. It was often said that 10 percent of the country's families held 90 percent of the wealth. The great majority of Filipinos were still poor, rural tenant farmers. What had made the problem worse was a huge increase in population. Although there was great poverty, there were more hospitals, more doctors, and more medicine, so fewer people died of disease. That meant there were larger numbers of people living on the tenant farms in the rural areas.

Many people believed the basic problem was still that the Philippines depended too much on the United States. The new president, Diosdado Macapagal, took some steps to increase the sense of Philippine independence from its large and powerful friend. One of the first things he did was to move Philippine Independence Day from July 4 to June 12, the date of the first Philippine declaration of independence in 1898. He also proposed a new plan to give more land to the landless tenant farmers. But the Philippine Congress included many representatives from landowning families, and it approved only limited reforms that would allow tenant farmers to share in some of the profits from the crops they grew. President Macapagal also had problems with corruption in his government, and by 1964, even though the next national elections were still a year away, opposing parties had already started campaigning against Macapagal.

Facing Macapagal in the 1965 election would be Senator Ferdinand Marcos, a strong and ambitious foe. Marcos, from the Ilocos region of northern Luzon, was the country's most decorated soldier from World War II. He had gained fame as a lawyer and had served first in the Philippine House of Representatives before winning election to the higher elective body, the Senate. He had started out with the Liberal party but had changed his allegiance to the Nacionalistas. He was clever, and he had spent his political career building strong friendships with important people in his province and throughout the Philippines. He also had a beautiful and ambitious wife, Imelda, who was from the province of Leyte and who made many appearances and speeches on behalf of her husband.

If the 1961 campaign had been vicious, the 1965 campaign was even dirtier and noisier, not to mention longer. And it was filled with corruption. One of the results of the extreme poverty in the Philippines was that many, many people were willing to sell their votes in elections. Representatives of candidates would hang around outside polling places and offer to buy votes, and the poor people would sell their votes to the highest bidder. Nobody seemed to be able to stop this practice. What it meant, of course, was that the candidate with the most money, or the most wealthy friends, could win. Even those people who refused to sell their votes did not always get to cast them. Especially in the rural areas, candidates would send thugs to beat up people who refused to vote their way. Or they would simply change the ballots so that the votes would be for their candidate, not his opponent. In the end, Marcos beat Macapagal by a large majority. That same election saw Benigno Aquino win a seat in the Philippine Senate on the Liberal party slate. Only in his mid-thirties, he became the youngest Filipino ever elected to the Senate.

By the time Marcos and Aquino took office, the unrest in the Philippines was worse than ever. Marcos stated in his first major speech to Congress that the country was in crisis, but he promised to lead it out of crisis. He tried to do more for the rural poor. He ordered the building of more roads and schools and irrigation facilities for the farmers. He got funding from the wealthy Rockefeller family in the United States to develop new varieties of rice that would grow faster and better, which would help feed the Philippine people and also give them more rice to sell to other countries. He helped form the Association of Southeast Asian Nations (ASEAN) with Thailand, Malaysia, Indonesia, and Singapore, which was aimed at improving trade and cultural cooperation. He was bright, had excellent ideas, and had the energy to put them into practice. In fact, some people hailed him as an Asian

John F. Kennedy, referring to the young U.S. president who had been assassinated in 1963 after less than three years in office.

Meanwhile, the First Lady, Imelda Marcos, was working to improve Philippine cultural pride by encouraging Philippine artists and dancers. Cultural centers—places where artists, writers, and dancers could work and show their work—were built under the Marcos administration.

Later, in 1971 during President Marcos's second term, he would form a commission to find tribes that still practiced ancient Filipino cultures and to protect them from being wiped out by modernization. This commission found the Tasaday, a very primitive tribe that lived in the mountain forests of the island of Mindanao. The Tasaday knew nothing of modern life. They did not hunt or farm. Instead, they gathered berries and fruits in the forests. They didn't even have words in their language for war or killing. They were a peaceful, gentle people, and President Marcos declared the area where they lived a protected place so that they could continue to live as they always had. He also set a national policy that would give such tribes the right to choose whether or not they wished to enter the modern world.

President Marcos introduced programs that helped the Philippine economy and that helped Filipinos to feel national pride. But his programs hardly scratched the surface of his country's problems. The huge gulf between rich and poor persisted—and that was the biggest problem. The majority of Filipinos were untouched by what the Marcoses did. What's more, Ferdinand Marcos's opponents charged that not only had he not done enough for the poor, he had used his office to make himself rich. As he drove to consolidate his power, he created a large group of men who owed allegiance to him in return for his favors. He gave his friends government jobs

Imelda Marcos was an active First Lady. She would become one of the most powerful women in the world.

and allowed them to form business monopolies. The more he helped his own family and friends, the less attention he paid to the poor. Unrest continued to grow. In the countryside, the Huks started to become strong again. So did the Moslems. Other guerrilla movements arose. Worse than the political rebels were the organized gangsters who committed murders and robberies and seemed to have the support of corrupt police and judges. Marcos could not seem to do much about them.

In 1969 Marcos ran for reelection as president against Senator Sergio Osmeña, Jr. Osmeña brought up the charge that Marcos had once been accused of murder. (This had actually happened, before World War II, and Marcos had been found not guilty.) He also accused Marcos of corruption and vote buying. Marcos accused Osmeña of collaborating with the Japanese during World War II (Osmeña had also been found not guilty of this charge) and of corruption and vote buying. Marcos won by a landslide and became the first president to be reelected since the Philippines became a republic in 1946.

For Marcos, his landslide victory meant that he was free to do what he wanted. For his opponents, it meant that he had won by vote buying and corruption and that he had too much power. Naturally, his opponents included the Liberal party, of which Benigno Aquino was a member, and which he served as a senator. But they also included many other Filipinos, organized and unorganized.

Even though the Philippine economy had improved under Marcos, the rapid increase of population reduced the effects of economic growth for the average Filipino. If ten people have to share a pie, and the pie gets bigger, then the ten people get more to eat. If the pie gets bigger but twenty people now have to share it, they wind up having less to eat. So, in the rural areas especially, there was more unrest than ever before, partly because the people expected things to be better and they were not. Farm groups engaged in a number of protests against the Marcos government, charging that it was not doing enough for them.

Labor groups also protested. So did student groups. Student protests first arose in the late 1960s when President Marcos sided with the United States in the war in Vietnam and even sent a Philippine construction and engineering battalion to South Vietnam. Like most of the student groups in the United States, the Philippine students believed that the war in Vietnam was a civil war and that neither the United States nor the Philippines should get involved in it. By the early 1970s the student groups that were against Marcos had a less specific cause: they believed that in general his was a corrupt government with too much power and that it used its power to benefit the rich, not the common people. In early 1970 thousands of young Filipinos took to the streets shouting, "Down with feudalism [land ownership only by the rich], fascism [one-party government], and imperialism [control of other nations]!" They marched to Congress and then to the presidential palace itself, and when they lit bonfires at the palace gates, the police fired upon them. Four people were killed, and nearly a hundred more were injured.

By this time, the demonstrators were a mixture of students, farmers, and laborers. Some were Moslems; many were Communists. They continued to march and now turned their attention to the United States embassy, throwing bombs and bottles and bricks at the building until U.S. Marines drove them away with tear gas. After each such demonstration, the protesters would quiet down for a time, but soon they would be back, in greater numbers. During 1970 and

1971 there were many such protests, sparked by all kinds of occurrences.

In 1971, an announced increase in the price of gasoline set off a protest by taxicab drivers. They were soon joined by students. They clashed with police, and there was so much violence that President Marcos announced he would postpone the price increases. But he also warned that unless things calmed down he would impose martial law.

Martial law is law by force. It is not democracy. In a democracy, government rules by the consent of the people. Under martial law, the people have no say in the matter. Even some of Marcos's supporters did not want martial law. His moderate critics certainly did not want it. They believed that there was a peaceful way to solve the problems of the Philippines. They realized that there was great unrest, but they also felt that Marcos was just making the situation worse by sending the police and the armed forces against protesters. They suspected that Marcos was using the protests as an excuse to change the form of government so that he would have more power.

Senator Benigno Aquino believed that this was just what President Marcos was doing. Chosen as the spokesman for the Liberal party, he made a powerful speech in which he insisted, "There is no rebellion; there is no invasion. There is really no imminent danger to the republic." Yes, there was opposition to the president, but the only danger was to Marcos and his party, not to the country.

For several months, the Marcos force for martial law and the Liberal opposition to it argued and debated with each other. Meanwhile, protests and violence continued by those who were not in power. The Liberal party gained strength at this time. In the 1971 senatorial elections, the party gained several seats in the Philippine Senate, although it did not win a majority. Benigno Aquino won reelection by a wide margin, and he was clearly a prime candidate to run against Marcos in the next presidential election in 1973. Public opinion polls showed that he had a very good chance of winning.

Actually, Ninoy Aquino would not be running against Ferdinand Marcos in 1973. Under the Philippine Constitution, as under the U.S. Constitution, a president could not run for a third consecutive term of office. President Marcos had decided to get around that problem by having his wife, Imelda, run for the presidency in his place.

But the 1973 presidential election was never held. Perhaps fearing that Aquino or some other opponent would win and facing the toppling of his empire, President Marcos decided to make sure there was no election. The unrest throughout the country provided him with a good excuse.

The year 1972 brought grave problems to the Philippines. Typhoons in July resulted in terrible floods that caused six hundred deaths, left two million homeless, and set back the economy by two years. In the disarray that followed, there were more terrorist attacks. On August 21 the Liberal party held an outdoor meeting in Manila to prepare for senatorial and local elections in November. Two grenades were thrown at the platform, killing seven spectators and injuring almost one hundred people. The injured included Senator Sergio Osmeña, the unsuccessful Liberal party candidate in the 1969 presidential elections, and Senator Jovito Salonga, who, like Benigno Aquino, was considered a strong contender for the party's presidential nomination. Senator Aquino was unhurt and declared that he held President Marcos responsible for failing to protect the citizens' right to hold assemblies.

Marcos responded by accusing Aquino of aiding Communist subversives by providing them with guns, ammunition, and other support. He said he had sworn statements from witnesses to Aquino's meetings with Communists, and two weapons, which he charged that Aquino had presented to Huk commanders.

Aquino called a press conference to deny the accusations. He challenged Marcos to bring legal charges against him and to prove them in court. As a senator, Aquino had "parliamentary immunity," which meant that he could not be charged with a crime. But he promised to give up that immunity. Marcos, he said, was "copying Hitler's tactics" by using anticommunism as an excuse to establish his own dictatorship.

On September 20, Defense Minister Juan Ponce Enrile issued a report that the Communist New People's Party was planning to bomb the presidential palace and start a revolution. Two days later, on September 22, Enrile was shot at as he rode in his car. That same evening, President Marcos sent military units to many parts of the Philippines. They shut down the Congress, the newspapers, and the radio and television stations. They took over airports and seaports and public utilities like the telephone and electricity. They arrested a number of officeholders, businessmen, and journalists—anyone who was regarded as an enemy. Among those who were arrested were the publisher of the *Manila Times,* Eugenio Lopez, Jr.; Sergio Osmeña III, grandson of the first vice-president of the Commonwealth of the Philippines; Luis Taruc, the former leader of the Huk guerrillas; and the secretary-general of the Liberal party, Benigno S. Aquino, Jr., the man who had persuaded Taruc to surrender twenty years earlier.

The following afternoon, Marcos ordered the captured radio and television stations opened so he could address the nation. In that speech, he explained that he had imposed martial law in order to save the nation. Referring to the attempt on

Juan Ponce Enrile was defense minister under Marcos. Later, he was the only former Marcos appointee to keep his job in the new Aquino government.

41

the life of Defense Minister Enrile, he charged that Communists had been about to take over the republic and that the only way to stop them had been to declare martial law. (Later, it came out that Marcos had signed the martial law order the day *before* the assassination attempt.) He promised that as soon as he had the national situation under control he would restore most of the freedoms that the Filipino people had come to expect.

Indeed, over the next few weeks and months, life for the average Filipino did return to normal in some ways. The military tanks and the armed soldiers left the streets and could be seen only at places like airports and passenger-ship docks. But Defense Minister Enrile warned in early November that if civilians did not cooperate with the president's reform program, the military would "take over the job." Newspapers started publishing again; radio and TV programs were back on the air. But the government had to approve what they wrote and broadcast, and the Filipino people knew that they were only getting the government's version of the news. Many of the people arrested and jailed were released. But the real leaders remained in jail, including Benigno S. Aquino, Jr.

Many people outside the Philippines marveled at how quickly and effectively Marcos had imposed martial law. They wondered why there was so little resistance. But Marcos had planned his action very well. He had jailed all the major leaders, and without their leaders the once-strong opposition became suddenly weak. Later, some people in the opposition explained that they had been caught by surprise when Marcos imposed martial law. Most of these people had grown up under democracy, and they didn't believe that Marcos would actually take such an undemocratic step. Martial law was something that dictators in nondemocratic countries did. They couldn't believe that it could happen in the Philippines. But it had happened.

5

Prisoners of the State

Cory Aquino will never forget the horror of her husband's arrest. Government soldiers invaded their home and took him away, refusing to tell her where they were taking him. One day soon after, they brought all her husband's personal effects to her—his clothes, his wallet, even his glasses—but refused to tell her whether he was dead or alive.

Frightened, not knowing what to do, Cory knew she would go mad if she simply stayed at home and waited. She decided that she would find her husband, dead or alive. Because so many thousands had been arrested by the Marcos forces, there were prison camps all over the Philippines. Cory began to visit them. Taking her infant daughter, Kris, she would approach a camp gate and ask if her husband was at the camp. Soldiers taunted her and made her sit outside like a beggar. On some days the sun beat down on her unmercifully. On other days, she sat in the pouring rain. But she refused to move until she got an answer. Finally, after forty-three days, she found her husband.

Ninoy Aquino had been taken north to Camp Laur and placed in solitary confinement. With no one to talk to, he thought he would go mad. All he had for company were his own thoughts, and they frightened him. He did not know if his wife and children were themselves in a prison camp. He did not know what was happening in the outside world. He paced his tiny cell and wondered how such a terrible thing could have happened to him. Then one day he saw a vision. He shook his head and blinked his eyes, but there it was—a vision of the Virgin Mary. Ninoy Aquino had never been very religious. In fact, he had teased his wife about her faith. Now he began to wonder if perhaps he had been wrong. Maybe there was more to life than what he had believed. He was terribly confused.

Once Cory Aquino learned where her husband was, she managed to get permission to see him. She gathered her five children and took them to Camp Laur. There they were taken to a barbed-wire fence. In his dark cell, Ninoy Aquino was surprised to see his guards open the door wide, and he was confused when they motioned to him to accompany them out of the cell. In the small, enclosed yard he blinked his eyes against the blinding light of day. Then, beyond the barbed wire, he saw his wife and children. He rushed to the fence. The children all began to cry, and Cory saw her husband break down and cry, too. In spite of her joy at seeing him, Cory was frightened by the change that had come over her husband. "That was the first time I saw Ninoy no longer the confident man I had always known," she said later. Cory wanted to cry, too, but she realized that someone had to be strong and that she had to be that someone. "Perhaps that was the greatest education of my life," Cory said years later. "In the past, I had always lived such a sheltered life, such a comfortable life."

Cory now began to visit every official she could think of in order to secure her husband's release from solitary confinement. She managed to get him moved from the prison camp to a detention center for political prisoners at Fort Bonifacio in Manila. She also got permission to visit him and endured the body search she had to go through before she was permitted to hold him in her arms.

She remembers that they cried together that first time they were permitted to embrace. "Why does it have to be us?" they asked each other. They had never harmed anyone. It didn't seem fair. Gradually, with the help of the faith they now shared, they were able to face their situation. Cory told an audience in 1984, "It wasn't until we got over the self-pity that we were able to accept suffering as part of our life with Christ."

For Cory Aquino, accepting their suffering did not mean doing nothing about it. She worked hard to make her husband's prison conditions better, and after a while her persistence was rewarded. He got his glasses back and was allowed to read newspapers and magazines. She sought, and won, the right to visit him more often and for longer periods of time. During her visits, she told him what was happening in the outside world. She became her husband's news service. And there was always much news to tell.

By the end of 1972, Marcos announced that the immediate danger from communism was over, and he began to release the people who had been arrested in September. He lifted some press restrictions. He ordered a special commission to write the new constitution and reorganized the government into local units called barangays that voted on national issues by raised hands. In early 1973 these barangays passed the new constitution. Opponents of Marcos argued that this was not legal and took the issue to the Philippine Supreme

Court. But the court, in a divided opinion, ruled that it was legal. Marcos declared the new constitution in effect on January 17, 1973. He promised to convene a new National Assembly as soon as he decided that it was in the best interests of the country. At that time, he did not believe it was. Marcos held all the power, and there was little that his opponents could do.

Benigno Aquino was convinced that someone had to fight against Marcos. He could do little himself from prison, but Cory could do something, and Cory was willing to act on her husband's behalf. The quiet housewife became her husband's representative outside the prison walls, and she did not just follow his instructions. She began to make decisions herself. "It was then that I finally came into my own," she said later. "I made all the major decisions; it was such a transformation."

On her husband's behalf, Cory contacted attorneys who specialized in civil rights and human rights cases. One of them, Joker Arroyo, became a particularly close friend. He and other attorneys brought suit against the government, charging that Marcos had acted illegally by declaring a new constitution in effect. Government attorneys kept trying to stall the case in court, but Cory persisted, refusing to give up. Finally, she took her case all the way to the Philippine Supreme Court. But she was not surprised when the court ruled in 1975 that Marcos had acted legally under both the old and the new constitution. The most difficult part for her was having to tell her husband that they had lost. She understood that the case had been a source of hope for him, something to keep him going.

She, too, needed something to fight for, something to keep her going. It was not easy for Cory Aquino during the years her husband was in prison. Her family and Ninoy's were

Benigno "Ninoy" Aquino was imprisoned for opposing the Marcos regime.

supportive. She was named treasurer of her family's company, José Cojuangco & Sons, and so earned a salary that enabled her to provide for her children. But many friends deserted her. People who had pretended to be good friends when they thought Ninoy would be the next president now carefully avoided her. Cory maintained her dignity and would smile when she saw these people on the street. But they would look away, or even cross the street so they wouldn't be seen with her. They believed that she was playing a dangerous game by being such an outspoken critic of Marcos. She knew she was. Her husband was still charged with murder. At any moment the government could take him to trial, find him guilty, and execute him. For that matter, at any moment she could be arrested for treason and sentenced to death.

Once the Supreme Court had decided against their case, Cory turned her energies to bringing more normalcy to their lives. She began to visit Marcos's minister of defense, Juan Ponce Enrile, to ask for increased visiting rights. Eventually she got permission to sleep at Fort Bonifacio every weekend. There was a mirror in her husband's cell, and they both suspected that it was a two-way mirror behind which the authorities spied on them. Cory insisted that a blanket be placed over the mirror. Then she got permission to have the children visit once a week. She decided that her husband ought to see other family members and the few friends who remained loyal to them. She presented Enrile with guest lists, which he approved or disapproved. Since Ninoy Aquino was still under indictment for murder and still regarded as an enemy of Marcos, it seems odd that Enrile would agree to these favors. But Cory was very persuasive, and Enrile came to respect the determined little woman who never gave up.

Cory got permission from Defense Minister Enrile to have the children sleep at the fort at Christmas and Easter. She and

Ninoy covered the stone floor of his cell with mattresses, and all five children slept with their parents. They pretended that they were camping out together, and the younger children lost their fear of the cold cell with its heavy metal door. The youngest child, Kris, remembers to this day that the peephole in the cell door was the magic place through which the "Christmas dwarf" brought presents.

As well-meaning as they had felt toward poor Filipinos, Ninoy and Cory Aquino had never really understood what it was like to try to be together under such conditions. Cory later explained, "Both of us were born privileged. We'd look at our maid and our driver and say that they'd never really had anything wonderful happen to them." Lying with their children on bare mattresses on the concrete floor of a cold prison cell at Christmastime, they came to realize that "wonderful" had nothing to do with money or other luxuries. It had to do with love and being together. They also understood that when even these things were denied to poor people with no food to eat, no roofs over their heads, and no medicines to treat their dying children, those poor people were not going to care very much about something called democracy. What they cared about was food, shelter, and medicine, and it didn't matter to them what kind of government gave it to them.

There were times when Ninoy and Cory despaired. In the outside world, Marcos was so powerful that he had stifled most opposition. Ninoy Aquino began to wonder if his prison cell had turned into a grave. "Are there people who still remember?" he would ask Cory. Cory realized that it was up to her to make them remember. She began to call press conferences to tell the Philippine people, and the rest of the world, that her husband was still alive and fighting. Her husband coached her carefully, telling her what questions might be asked and how to answer them. At first, she was very nervous, but after a while, she later explained, she "got the hang of it."

President Marcos did not like what Cory was doing. But he did not want to overreact. He was firmly in command and did not want to seem frightened by one little woman talking to the press about her imprisoned husband. He let the press conferences go on for about two years before he decided he'd had enough. Benigno Aquino was becoming a kind of national hero. Marcos decided it was time to bring him to trial.

In 1977 a military court convicted Aquino of all the charges against him and sentenced him to death in front of a firing squad. While both Ninoy and Cory had expected the verdict, it was nevertheless a shock to hear it. But once again they decided to act. Ninoy went on a hunger strike. For forty days he refused all solid food. Cory was allowed to visit him. She brought thermoses of liquid filled with vitamins. She also hid notes in the thermoses. She kept him alive, but just barely. After forty days he was so weak that Marcos ordered him hospitalized.

For all his power, Marcos did have the United States to answer to. It was U.S. aid that kept the Philippine economy going. The United States had continued to support Marcos even after he had imposed martial law because he insisted that his country was threatened by the Communists. The one thing the United States feared more than anything else was communism, and U.S. officials were willing to overlook many of Marcos's actions as long as they believed he was an ally against communism. But even the United States was bothered by Marcos's continued violations of human rights and by the rising criticism from all sectors of the Philippine people. By 1979, Cardinal Jaime Sin, archbishop of Manila, was outspoken in his criticism of martial law. He said that the people

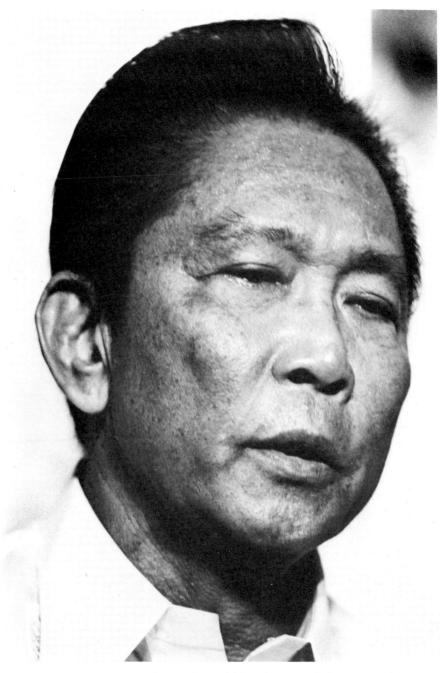

Ferdinand Marcos said he imposed martial law because of the communist threat. His critics said he was afraid of losing his power.

51

had no confidence in politicians, the armed forces, or the courts and that many Filipinos had lost all hope of a peaceful solution.

Among those who had not lost this hope was Benigno Aquino. He believed that violent civil war would ruin the Philippines. In October 1979, through Cory, he sent a proposal to President Marcos. In it he called for a three-year plan leading up to general elections and the ending of martial law by January 1983. In the meantime, a council of leaders representing all sectors of society would advise the president. Marcos did not immediately answer Aquino about the proposal.

People in the United States knew that Marcos had Aquino in prison because he was his strongest political enemy. They would not stand still and allow Marcos to execute Aquino or let him die in prison. After Aquino was hospitalized, Marcos was forced to revoke the order of execution.

Aquino recovered from most of the effects of his hunger strike, but the long years in prison and forty days without solid food had weakened his heart. Cory worried that he would eventually die in prison anyway, of a heart attack. She now campaigned for better medical attention for her husband. She got outside doctors to treat him, but even they could do little about his worsening condition.

Cory called a press conference. If her husband remained in prison, he would surely die, she told reporters. The last thing Marcos wanted was a dead hero for his opposition to rally around. In December 1979, Aquino was allowed to go home on extended Christmas leave, but he remained under house arrest. It had been seven years and seven months since Marcos's soldiers had taken him away.

The Aquino family rejoiced in their first Christmas together at home in all that time. They tried not to think about the future, for they did not know how long Marcos's holiday spirit would last. A less courageous man than Ninoy Aquino would have cooperated with Marcos or at least would have kept his mouth shut. Benigno Aquino did neither.

On January 8, 1980, the *Bangkok Post* published an interview with Marcos. He said that, in order to help the country out of a serious crisis, he was ready to establish a "council of leaders" such as former Senator Aquino had proposed. He added during a television interview the following night that Aquino himself would be offered a seat on the council. Reporters went to the Aquino home in the suburbs of Manila to find out the former senator's reaction. Aquino said he would prefer not to serve on such a council but would do so, if asked, on the minimum condition that a free press would be established.

Marcos was disappointed by what Aquino had to say. Shortly afterward, Aquino's "extended Christmas leave" was declared ended, and he was returned to prison. Meanwhile, on January 30, the first elections for local officials in the Philippines since 1971 were held. Marcos had formed a new party, the New Society Movement, and most of its candidates won. Benigno Aquino's old friend Salvador Laurel, who had once been a supporter of Marcos, had joined with others to form a new party of their own—the United Democratic Opposition, or UNIDO Most of its candidates lost, which did not surprise anyone who knew how the powerful Marcos could rig elections.

As closely as she followed the elections, Cory was more concerned about her husband. After having him home for that brief time, she could not bear to lose him again. She was also extremely worried about his health. His doctors said he needed triple bypass heart surgery, and she wanted the operation performed by expert surgeons. She asked permission for the operation to be done in the United States. In May, Marcos, under pressure from his own advisers and from U.S. officials, granted permission for Aquino and his family to go to Dallas, Texas, for the surgery. He expected that Aquino would remain in the United States, and he felt that his opponent would be less threatening and less influential if he was far away.

6

Exile—
And a Tragic Homecoming

The operation was successful. After he recovered, Ninoy Aquino did remain in the United States with his family. One reason was that Marcos had issued another order for his arrest. From August to October there was a series of bomb explosions in Manila. One of them, on October 9, occurred at a meeting of American travel agents that President Marcos was addressing. The next day Marcos ordered the arrest of thirty people, including four former senators. Three of them, including Benigno Aquino, were in the United States at the time. The fourth, Jovito Salonga, was held in custody for a time and then placed under house arrest.

Aquino moved his family to Massachusetts, where he obtained research fellowships at Harvard and the Massachusetts Institute of Technology. The family moved into a house in Boston, and the children enrolled in local schools. For the first time in her life, Cory did not have a maid to do her housework, but she happily dusted and scrubbed, for at long last she had her husband back and her family together again.

She sometimes had to pinch herself to realize that he was no longer in a cold prison cell, that she could reach out and touch him whenever she wanted to and no longer had to wait for the official weekly visit. Her children finally had their father back.

For this reason, too, she tried not to feel resentment when her husband once again began to make all the decisions for the family. After nearly eight years, she had become accustomed to making such decisions, and it was not easy to step back into her husband's shadow. But part of her was relieved about giving up that burden, and most of her believed in the tradition that the husband made the decisions. She later recalled that the years in Boston were the happiest of her life.

Ninoy Aquino was also happy. He had his family back. He had his health back, and he had his freedom. He could speak without worrying about listening devices. But he missed the Philippines, and he worried about what was happening in his beloved native land.

In January 1981 President Marcos at last lifted martial law and proposed to hold a presidential election in May to seek a renewed mandate as the candidate of his own New Society Movement. This excited Benigno Aquino, who announced from Boston that he was prepared to return to the Philippines to campaign for UNIDO candidates if Marcos would allow him freedom of movement or full access to the media from prison if he were arrested. Aquino himself was not eligible to run because he was only forty-eight years old, and the Marcos constitution had a minimum age of fifty for the presidency. But the leaders of UNIDO decided that the election was a farce and refused to participate, so Aquino did not return.

He did, however, travel to Tokyo, Japan, in April to meet with Salvador Laurel and others to discuss the possibility of joining forces with Moslem rebels in the southern Philippines. The following month he traveled to Saudi Arabia. Marcos charged that, while there, Aquino discussed a plot to assassinate Marcos. Aquino insisted that he had made the trip "at the request of the Philippine government" to try to negotiate an end to the conflict in the southern islands.

Meanwhile, on May 4, a military court put off a decision on the death sentence that had been passed on Aquino back in November 1977.

After running practically unopposed in his presidential election, Ferdinand Marcos was inaugurated for a new six-year term in office on June 30, 1981. The ceremony was attended by U.S. Vice President George Bush, who promised full U.S. support to the Philippines and its non-Communist neighbors. In the eyes of the United States government, Marcos was the best hope against communism in that part of the world, and so it managed to ignore his abuses of democracy and human rights. For his part, Marcos was quite pleased with the way he had handled things and later that year even reminded his absent enemy, Benigno Aquino, that he was still boss. Aquino's lawyers had appealed his death sentence to the Philippine Supreme Court since 1977. Marcos said he believed that when the court finally considered the appeals it would deny them. He preferred to wait for that to happen. But, "if necessary," he would himself reverse his "staying order" and reinstate the death sentence.

Unable to return to his native land, Ninoy Aquino found himself paying more attention to the fight against dictatorships in other parts of the world. He traveled to Nicaragua and to Lebanon and in both countries saw the ravages of civil war. As much as he hated what Marcos had done to the Philippines, he did not want his country to suffer the same fate. Not just his religious faith but his sense of political realism caused him to believe that the best course for the Philippines was nonviolence.

President Marcos and his family posed for this portrait following his inauguration on June 30, 1981. At the time, Benigno Aquino and his family were in exile in the United States.

Meanwhile, he and Cory kept a close watch on events in the Philippines. They were heartened by the increasingly activist role taken there by the Catholic Church, especially by Cardinal Jaime Sin. Cardinal Sin had charged the Marcos government with a deliberate attempt to silence the Church in the May 1981 presidential election campaign. In July 1982 he called for the resignation of President Marcos, saying that the corruption of his government had done more than anything else to strengthen the Communists. When asked if he wasn't getting more deeply involved in politics than a churchman should, Cardinal Sin replied, "The Church has to guide our people and in guiding them has to creep into politics occasionally."

Ninoy and Cory were also happy to learn of the increasing problems for Marcos, even though those problems were also hurting their country. The Communist insurgency was stronger than ever. The economy was worse off than ever. Marcos's opponents charged that U.S. aid was going into the pockets of the president and Mrs. Marcos and their friends, not to the country and its people. Ninoy was convinced that if something were not done soon, no one would be able to save the Philippines.

By the end of December 1982 he had a plan. He would return to the Philippines and persuade Marcos to step down. He would talk Marcos into the idea of making history as a great dictator who walked away from his power in favor of democracy and the good of his country. In return, he, Benigno S. Aquino, Jr., who had opposed Marcos for years, would support Marcos. In so doing, he would ruin his own political future, because other enemies of Marcos would call him a "collaborationist." He understood that, but he believed it was necessary for the good of the Philippines.

Cory did not share her husband's idealism. She did not believe that Marcos would consent to leave office under any circumstances. She asked her husband, "Are you prepared to accept imprisonment the second time around?" Ninoy said he was. Cory looked at him and remembered the first time. She wondered how he could put himself, not to mention her and the children, through such an experience again. But as she looked at him she also saw the determination in his eyes, and she knew she could not change his mind. She said, "So the matter is settled. We will go back."

Idealistic as he was, Ninoy Aquino understood the dangers of his decision. He told Cory that he would go back first alone. If all went well, then she and the children would join him a few days later. So Cory helped her husband make plans to return to the country where a death sentence hung over his head.

Ninoy Aquino applied for renewal of his Philippine passport. His application was turned down. Representatives of the Marcos government contacted Aquino to arrange a secret meeting in New York with the president's wife.

Over the years, Imelda Marcos had become more and more important in her husband's administration. Her role grew even larger after her husband began to suffer from a kidney ailment. They both constantly denied that there was anything wrong with the president, but there were some reports that the First Lady already had posters printed for her own campaign to succeed her husband as president.

The Marcoses had a townhouse and a number of business properties in New York City, and Imelda Marcos often traveled there to shop. She was very much in familiar territory when she met secretly in May with Benigno Aquino. At that meeting, she warned him that he should not return to the

Philippines. She said the Marcos government could not guarantee his safety, which Aquino understood as a hidden threat that an attempt would be made on his life. The First Lady offered him a "financially secure position in business" if he stayed away from Philippine politics.

Benigno Aquino refused to be bribed. In fact, he was so angry that he decided that he would not support Marcos under any circumstances. He decided instead to form a new political party, called Laban ("Fight"). Many of his friends in the Philippines were eager to help set up this party. But his old friend Salvador Laurel preferred to stay with UNIDO, the coalition of opposition parties that he had founded.

Cory's brother José helped to set up Laban. Its color was yellow. Its official sign was an *L* made with the thumb and forefinger. Cory had great hopes for the new party, for her husband, and for their life together. Recently, she had tried her hand at writing the short poems called haiku. In early June, she wrote this verse:

> The worst of my life
> Is over, I hope, And may
> The best please come soon.

"I remember when I read it to Ninoy," she said later. "He said, 'I don't think you've experienced the worst yet. There is so much we have to do.'"

It was no coincidence that on July 31, soon after the formation of Laban, the Philippine military court that had first sentenced Benigno Aquino to death confirmed the sentence and stated that if he returned to the Philippines he would be arrested.

Aquino took this threat seriously. He understood that Ferdinand Marcos considered him his greatest enemy. But he refused to back down. On August 7 he announced that he would return home even though he had been officially warned that there were plots to murder him (he was referring to what Mrs. Marcos had told him) and that he should stay in the United States for at least another month until those plots were investigated. He said he did not intend to wait. "I would rather die a glorious death," he joked, "than be killed by a Boston taxicab."

He was no fool. He did take a few precautions. But he was playing a dangerous game. He obtained a forged passport in the name Marcial Bonifacio (Andres Bonifacio had been a hero of an early Philippines independence movement, and Ninoy had been imprisoned in Fort Bonifacio). He traveled to the Philippines by way of Japan, Hong Kong, and Taiwan. As his plane from Taiwan approached Manila Airport on August 21, 1983, he put on a bulletproof vest. Everyone knew he was coming. Waiting at the airport were representatives of the international press and a welcoming committee headed by his old friend Salvador Laurel. Also waiting were fifteen soldiers who had been sent to arrest him.

As the plane touched down, Ninoy Aquino took a last look at the speech he had written, in which he said he was returning home "to restore our rights and freedoms through nonviolence." He never had a chance to give that speech. As he descended the stairs from the Taiwan airliner, a shot rang out. Benigno Aquino fell, face down, to the ground. The bulletproof vest had offered no protection for his head. He was killed instantly.

Almost immediately, more shots were heard, and another man met his death on the runway at Manila Airport. The entire scene was caught by Japanese television and broadcast to the world. Back in Boston, Cory Aquino and her children watched in horror.

Benigno Aquino was assassinated at Manila International Airport upon his return from exile in the United States. The bullet-proof vest he wore offered no protection for his head.

Two Japanese journalists on board the airliner said on the very day of the killing that they had seen soldiers pull their pistols and fire at Aquino's head. But the official version of the killing (put out by the Marcos government) was that Aquino had been shot by a man in the uniform of an airport worker and that the killer had in turn been shot to death by three of the fifteen soldiers sent to arrest Aquino. The authorities did not identify the killer until August 30, when they gave his name as Rolando Galman y Dawang and stated that he was a professional killer.

For Cory Aquino, the only fact that was important was that her husband was dead. She had feared that it would happen, and it had. This time there would be no visiting hours; he was gone. She had to be strong. She had to go to Manila to claim her husband's body and preside over the funeral.

In Manila, in spite of her grief, she was heartened by the reaction of the Filipino people. During the ten days of mourning, some two million people filed past Ninoy's body or accompanied it to the funeral. Cory wished that Ninoy could have known how much the people loved him.

At the same time, she was astonished at how the people seemed to love her. She understood that as the widow of a slain hero, she somehow was a symbol of him. But it surprised her when some people called for her to take Ninoy's place as Marcos's rival. She tried to stop such talk, saying, "I know my limitations, and I don't like politics. I was only involved because of my husband." But she did nothing to try to stop the talk that Marcos had ordered her husband's death. She believed that with all her heart. She tried not to hate Marcos, but she could not help remembering that he had made her family miserable for most of the past eleven years. She could not help despairing that Ninoy had died for nothing.

Cory and her children returned to the Philippines for Ninoy's funeral.

When no one seemed to believe the official report on the Aquino assassination, Marcos announced that he was appointing a commission to investigate the murder. The commission did not meet until September 5. They wanted the Aquino family to testify. Cory and her in-laws refused to take part in the commission's work, and so did Cardinal Jaime Sin. They charged that the commission would only try to cover up the government's guilt.

Salvador Laurel announced that his UNIDO party would boycott all future elections unless Marcos resigned. Laban, the new political party that Aquino had started, also demanded Marcos's resignation and promised a series of nonviolent demonstrations against the government. Cory's brother José asked her to take part in those demonstrations, and she agreed.

The seven-member commission appointed by Marcos to investigate the murder announced on October 1 that the accused killer, Galman, was a Communist guerrilla commander and that Aquino's "execution" had been ordered by the chairman of the Communist party of the Philippines. But most members of the commission were obviously pressured to issue that report. The chairman resigned. The man who was supposed to succeed him refused the chairmanship. Four other members resigned. Marcos announced the formation of a new commission, but he could get only four people to serve on it. Two weeks later, the U.S. House of Representatives called on Marcos to carry out a thorough, impartial, and swift investigation into the murder, to restore freedom of the press, and to ensure free and fair elections to the National Assembly in May.

Every day there were mass demonstrations in the streets. By now, Marcos was used to them. But he was not used to the new kinds of people who were taking part in these demonstrations. They were middle-class people, business people. Some two hundred thousand people of all classes demonstrated in Manila on November 27, which would have been Benigno Aquino's forty-ninth birthday. Marcos called them all "Communists."

There was no question that Ferdinand Marcos was "running scared." In fact, Salvador Laurel changed his mind about boycotting the elections to the National Assembly in May 1984. He was not alone. Cardinal Jaime Sin urged people to vote against anyone who was in league with Marcos, and three days later so did Cory Aquino. She wanted Marcos to be defeated without bloodshed. In taking this stand, she went against her brother-in-law, Agapito "Butz" Aquino. Ninoy's brother wanted the people to revolt against Marcos. He would not take part in Marcos-ordered elections.

Once again, the elections were neither free nor fair. Friends and supporters of Marcos won election to the National Assembly through fraud and vote buying. Unrest among the people continued to grow.

In October 1984 the second commission to investigate the death of Benigno Aquino concluded that the killing was the result of a "military conspiracy." They rejected unanimously the earlier commission's claim that Rolando Galman had killed Aquino. What they could not agree on was who in the military was responsible. A few said it was the chief of aviation security. The majority believed that the conspiracy had involved several top military men, including the chief of staff of the armed forces, General Fabian Ver. The majority ruled, and the following February twenty-six military men, including General Ver, went on trial.

Many military officers, active and retired, were embarrassed and ashamed. They felt that the actions of a few had

Cory urged anti-Marcos protesters to defeat the dictator without violence.

"cast a stigma" on the Philippine armed forces as a whole.

That fall of 1984, Cory Aquino briefly became an activist. She had been sickened by the rigged elections in the spring. She believed that if Marcos's own commission could find his military men guilty, then Marcos was in trouble. She decided it was time to act. On October 25, with Ninoy's brother Butz, she led a march of ten thousand people through Manila to demand the resignation of Marcos. Five days later a similar demonstration was broken up by riot police using water cannons, tear gas, and clubs. Disturbed that she had led people into danger, Cory backed off. She decided that it was better to try to negotiate.

In December she joined with former Senator Lorenzo Tanada to form the Convenors Group. The name referred to the convening, or getting together, of people who wanted to do something about the corrupt government. They demanded a new constitution, the legalization of the Communist party, the removal of foreign military bases, and a review of the Marcos government's economic treaties and financial agreements. They also called for new presidential elections. Almost every opposition leader formally agreed with these demands. The exception was Salvador Laurel. He did not agree with the demand to remove U.S. military bases.

By this time there was wide speculation that President Marcos might be forced at last to call for open presidential elections. The Convenors Group issued a list of eleven candidates. Salvador Laurel announced that he, too, would be a candidate. There was wide speculation that Imelda Marcos, not her husband, would run. Ferdinand Marcos was obviously in failing health and made few public appearances. But 1985 wore on, and the Marcos government did not call for a presidential election.

7

Campaign

There was no question that the Marcos government was in trouble. The real question was whether the various forces opposing Marcos could take advantage of the situation. They were deeply divided. There were the Communists on the left. There were the anti-Communists on the right. And then there was the vast center. They needed one strong leader to unite behind. Benigno Aquino might have been that leader. By the fall of 1985 many people were beginning to look to his widow as the only person who was far enough above the political differences that divided the opposition. Cory, for her part, was beginning to take that idea seriously.

In October 1985 she was invited to speak in front of a University of the Philippines sorority on the topic "My Role as Wife, Mother, and Single Parent." During the question-and-answer period that followed, students begged her to declare herself a candidate against Marcos. The answer was out of Cory's mouth almost before she knew it: Yes, all right, she would stand for the presidency—*if* President Marcos called an election and *if* one million Filipinos signed petitions in support of her candidacy.

When he heard what Cory had said, Ferdinand Marcos laughed. He could not imagine that a housewife, as he called Cory, would even consider running against him. Besides, he had no intention of calling for an election. Within a month, however, he had changed his mind.

The Philippine economy was a shambles. The Communists were gaining strength daily. The Moslem rebels in Mindanao were at it again. And U.S. officials had made it clear that if he did not do something soon, he would lose even U.S. support. In November, Marcos surprised his own advisers by calling a "snap election" for February of the following year.

Cory's supporters got busy right away. Women's groups were particularly strong in backing her candidacy, and they went out in droves with petitions. One month later they presented her with a petition signed by one million Filipinos asking her to run. During that month, Cory began to prepare for her candidacy. There was a lot she had to learn—and quickly—about politics and government. Advisers from the University of the Philippines, from business, and from the media were eager to help. So were her brother José and the other leaders of Laban. And so were Joker Arroyo and the other attorneys who had done so much to help Ninoy during his long years in prison. These men tried to persuade her that she really had a chance to beat Marcos. But Cory, though she went through the motions of preparing for her candidacy, remained unconvinced.

She believed she had the support of many in the middle class, especially the women, although she did not publicly boast of that support, not wishing to put off Filipino men. She was not sure about the vast majority of poor, uneducated Filipinos. While Ninoy was in prison, she had come to understand what it was like to sleep on a bare mattress on a cold prison cell floor, what it was like to have no power over her life. But she also understood that she had looked at this situation from the perspective of a comfortable, educated background. The poor were too busy worrying about where their next meal was coming from to worry about much else. She remembered what Bertrand Russell had said. This famous mathematician had become a peace activist in his later years and had decided that what would bring peace to the world was enough for the world to eat. He had asked, "If one man offers you democracy and another offers you a bag of grain, at what stage of starvation will you prefer the grain to the vote?" Cory asked, Did the poor understand things like truth, justice, and freedom? Her advisers were unable to convince her that they did.

Cory did not feel she could beat Marcos unless she had the support of the poor people. She could just imagine Marcos handing out money and food and buying votes as usual.

When her advisers could not persuade her otherwise, she became impatient with them. In reality, though, she was impatient with herself. It was she who could not make a decision. She turned to prayer. She went to church and prayed as she had never prayed before, saying, "Please, Lord, tell me what to do."

After mass one Sunday in early November, Cory had lunch with Monsignor Orlando Panlican. She asked him the same question that she had been asking herself and everyone around her: Can the poor people understand ideas like truth, justice, and freedom? "Yes, they can," the priest answered. He explained that if they could understand Marcos as a symbol of evil and suffering, then they could also understand that someone else was a symbol of goodness and justice.

There, at last, was an answer that Cory Aquino could understand. "We had to present somebody who was the complete opposite of Marcos," she said later, "someone who had been a victim." And she knew who that could be: "Looking around, I may not be the worst victim, but I am the best known."

For the next three weeks, Cory prepared for her candidacy with excitement and a real feeling that she might be able to win. She talked with her advisers about campaign issues and speeches and about how to deal with other opposition leaders. She managed to get the support of eight opposition parties. But the Communists refused to participate in the election. And the extreme anti-Communists also refused to support her. Salvador Laurel would not support her either, for he was intent on running for the presidency himself. Cory did not want to run against someone like Laurel. In fact, she asked him if he would run as her vice-president, but he refused.

Cory asked her daughters to help her shop for yellow fabric (yellow, as mentioned, was the color of the Laban party) and to make dresses for her to wear as she campaigned. Those dresses were going to be important. Cory even got yellow-rimmed eyeglasses. If all went well, the color yellow would come to symbolize the sunlight she wanted to bring into the darkness of the Philippines under Marcos.

On Monday, December 2, all twenty-six military men accused of conspiracy in the death of Benigno Aquino were acquitted by a special tribunal. Marcos immediately reinstated General Fabian Ver as chief of staff of the armed forces and promised a complete reorganization of the military.

On Tuesday, December 3, Marcos officially signed a law setting up a special presidential election for February 7, 1986. Just a few hours later, Maria Corazon Cojuangco Aquino announced at a special press conference: "I hereby affirm my candidacy and confirm my willingness to serve our people as president of the Republic of the Philippines."

Corazon Aquino, candidate for president of the Philippines, at a rally
with her vice-presidential running mate, Salvador Laurel (right).

Salvador Laurel had not really believed that Cory would go through with it. Once she had, he changed his mind about running with her. In spite of himself he came to believe, as she did, that the best way to beat Marcos was to present a person completely opposite from him. Cory Aquino, fifty-two-year-old widow of a national martyr, dressed in sunny yellow and smiling, was that person. Urged on by many in the opposition, as well as by Cardinal Jaime Sin, he met again with Cory and her advisers. After they promised that he would have real power in the new Aquino government if they won, and after they promised to run as the candidates of his UNIDO party, he agreed to run as her vice-president. They reached their agreement only an hour before the midnight deadline for officially filing their candidacy and hurried to file before the deadline. In the space headed OCCUPATION, Cory wrote "housewife."

There were many ways in which Cory Aquino was the opposite of Ferdinand Marcos. These included the organization and financing of their campaigns. Marcos had a strong political machine throughout the Philippines. He also controlled all the national media. When he wanted to make an appearance, his local supporters made sure that huge crowds were brought by bus to cheer him (often the people in these crowds were actually paid to come). His campaign appearances were big shows, with convoys of limousines and entertainment by television personalities. Often the First Lady, Imelda Marcos, would sing for the crowds. It was said that Marcos had a campaign fund of $160 million.

By contrast, Cory and her running mate, "Doy" Laurel, raised about $25 million in campaign contributions. They could not count on attracting crowds when they traveled around the islands because Marcos allowed almost no media coverage of the Aquino campaign. She had trouble even buying advertising time. She finally filed suit against the government-owned Channel 4 in Manila to force increased coverage of her campaign. The channel mentioned her only four times in the next three days.

Toward the end of the campaign she got television attention she did not want. Marcos supporters created ads that showed her standing in front of scenes of war and chaos. She complained bitterly about these ads, but they were not stopped.

When she and Laurel campaigned, they usually rode through the streets of a town in the back of a truck. If anyone sang, it was Cory's fifteen-year-old daughter Kristina. Cory's candidacy was still so new, as was her partnership with Laurel, that they hadn't even had time to organize. But that did not stop them.

Of course, Cory's campaign platform was also vastly different from that of Marcos. He had been in power so long that there were few new issues he could talk about. He was in the uncomfortable position of having to defend his administration. Rather than talk about issues, he attacked Cory personally, saying that the only place for a woman was in the bedroom. He also made promises and spent a great deal of money. He increased salaries in the armed forces, gave out cash Christmas bonuses to more than a million civilian government workers, and reduced the cost of electricity in rural areas. He also headed off the long-simmering speculation that his wife would succeed him as president if he died. He chose as his vice-presidential running mate Arturo Tolentino, a longtime critic whom Marcos had once fired as foreign minister. By this choice, Marcos hoped to show that he was truly interested in reform.

Cory waves to her supporters from a campaign motorcade. Her candidacy inspired many ordinary Filipinos.

Cory had all sorts of issues to talk about, because so much had gone wrong in the Philippines under Marcos. She questioned his heroic war record: Marcos had always said that he had led a group of resistance fighters against the Japanese during World War II. Cory pointed out that no one had ever been able to prove his claims. She spoke out against the corruption of his government, ending each speech with the slogan "Sobra na, tama na, palitan na!" ("Too much, enough, let's change!"). She promised to bring free enterprise to the Philippines and to break up the business monopolies that Marcos had allowed his friends to build. She promised to renegotiate the terms of her country's foreign debt so the Philippines would have a longer time to pay off the huge amounts owed.

She promised to do all she could to bring peace to the Philippines. She offered to make peace with the Moslems on Mindanao. She also offered to negotiate with the Communist insurgents, provided that they laid down their arms. In early January she went so far as to say, "So long as the Communists renounce all forms of violence, we welcome them into our government."

Once Cory made that statement, Ferdinand Marcos knew exactly what the theme of his campaign would be: the threat of communism. During much of his career he had used anticommunism as an excuse for his actions—for declaring martial law, for not holding elections, for refusing to share power. And he had ensured the support of the United States by his anti-communist stand. Now Cory Aquino was inviting the Communists into her government!

Marcos claimed that Cory's brother-in-law, Agapito "Butz" Aquino, was a Communist and that there were other Communists among her advisers. He never went so far as to accuse Cory Aquino of being a Communist. He didn't give her that much credit. He continued to call her a housewife who should have stayed at home. But he suggested that she was under the influence of Communists and called her a "helpless tool" and a "mouthpiece." He would ask at rallies, "Can we take a chance on her at this crucial time for our country and our people?"

These charges infuriated Cory. She demanded that Marcos prove them, that he either "put up or shut up" and that he "stand up like a woman and tell the truth." She insisted, "It is the people who are supporting me, not the Americans, not the Communists."

As election day drew near, Cory's campaign gained momentum. The crowds were bigger, the cheering louder. The color yellow was everywhere—on banners and signs and people's clothing. So was the L hand signal. Cory was more relaxed and confident in her campaign speeches. But the same sincerity remained. She had caught the imagination of the Filipino people, and they began to believe that she really could beat Marcos.

Cardinal Jaime Sin did not feel it was right for him to endorse a presidential candidate. But it was clear whom he supported when he said, "I am tempted to ask, Is this a presidential election, or is this a contest between the forces of good and evil?" He, too, believed that the poor Filipino majority could understand that, even if they could not understand the idea of democracy.

Meanwhile, the Marcos campaign seemed to have little spark at all. In spite of the efforts of his local workers, the president did not draw huge, enthusiastic crowds anymore. Nor did he seem to have the strength to inspire the people. He appeared weak and feeble, and at times he rambled on about communism almost as if he were talking to himself.

Cory gives the "L" sign for *Laban*, meaning "fight."

There was no question that he was in trouble, and as the prospect loomed that he might actually lose the election, his forces went to work to make sure he won it.

Aquino workers began to receive threats against their lives. There was vote buying and fraud, which was nothing new under Marcos. Cory brought the issue of fraud out into the open. Marcos answered by inviting a group of "official observers" from the United States to be present in the Philippines to see that the election was open and honest. Marcos also allowed the American news media to cover the election. Cory hoped that the presence of outsiders would help.

8

People's Power

On election day twenty-four million Filipinos voted in the first "free" presidential election in sixteen years. Cory went to her native Tarlac Province to cast her ballot. "Today is my day," she told reporters. "I hope to see you at my inaugural." It is not known how many would-be voters were denied that right, or whose votes were "lost" and never counted. There were many reports of vote buying, physical violence, even the actual stealing of ballot boxes. Observers, official and unofficial, disagreed on how much fraud there was. With polling places located throughout the seven thousand islands, it was impossible to watch them all.

What was beyond dispute was that most of the fraud and violence occurred on the Marcos side. In the remote province of Antique, Aquino's local campaign director, Evelio Javiar, was shot to death. By the time the voting was over, 156 people, nearly all of them members of the opposition, had been killed in the campaign. On election day, Aquino supporters were attacked as they tried to protect ballot boxes. In some pro-Marcos provinces, ridiculous vote tallies like twelve thousand to zero were reported.

At the Marcos-controlled Philippine National Assembly in Manila, large green tote boards were set up to record the votes. Brown envelopes from each of the voting centers were opened and the results read aloud and then chalked onto the boards. Much of the time the room was in chaos as charges flew back and forth that envelopes were improperly sealed, that entire towns were not represented, that impossible tallies were being reported. When the totals consistently showed Marcos ahead, some of the election clerks began to wonder what was going on. The results on the tote boards didn't match the results in the envelopes. Some of the clerks, Marcos government employees, walked out in protest.

The U.S. delegation of official observers was outraged, but in Washington, D.C., President Ronald Reagan and his advisers were not prepared to move against Marcos. They did not believe that Cory Aquino was capable of being president of the Philippines. President Reagan stated that there had been fraud "on both sides," even though there was no evidence at all of tampering by Aquino people. Cory accused Reagan of "leaning in favor of election theft."

On February 9, two days after the election, Marcos announced that he was the winner by thirteen million votes to eleven million votes. Almost immediately, Cory announced that she was the winner, saying, "The people and I have won and we know it." Meanwhile, the members of the National Assembly had yet to certify anyone as the winner. When they certified Marcos the winner by eleven million to nine million votes, Cory felt betrayed.

She had every right to feel that way. She was positive that by any accurate count she had won. If she bowed to defeat, she would be letting down all the people who had worked for and voted for her. She refused to give up the fight. Instead, she called a giant rally in Manila and a thirteen-mile protest

84

After the voting in the special February 1986 election, Cory was confident that she would win. "This is my day," she told reporters.

parade to launch a "People's Victory" campaign of nonviolent resistance and boycotts around the country.

✓ The Catholic bishops of the Philippines would take part in these demonstrations. The 104-member Catholic Bishops Conference had not publicly supported either Marcos or Aquino. But they believed Marcos had now gone too far and had stolen the election. In the middle of February the bishops issued a strongly worded statement declaring that "a government that assumes or maintains power through fraudulent means has no moral basis." In that statement, they also issued a call for a "nonviolent struggle for justice." This was a powerful call in a country that is 85 percent Catholic.

The bishops, and Cory Aquino, understood that they had to act. If the moderate forces opposing Marcos did not act, then the Communists and other radicals on the left, not to mention the conservatives on the right, would move in to exploit the people's sense of frustration and betrayal over Marcos's victory. But in such a highly charged atmosphere, even a nonviolent campaign could turn violent. It could quickly turn into a full-scale, armed revolution. Cory prayed that she and the bishops could keep their People's Victory campaign under control.

Cory's boycott call led to heavy withdrawals from seven banks owned by Marcos's friends and associates. A large beverage corporation owned by a friend of Marcos saw a huge drop in business. Two thousand students poured into the streets of Manila and burned progovernment newspapers. They also asked people not to watch the government-owned Channel 4 TV station.

Ferdinand Marcos may have been privately worried about these events, but publicly he paid no attention to them. He had, after all, been declared the winner of the election by the National Assembly. But when Cory set about holding a series of People's Victory rallies, Marcos was furious. He hinted that if the demonstrations did not stop he would call out the army to put them down.

Then, on February 22, an action occurred that took both sides by surprise. Defense Minister Juan Ponce Enrile and Deputy Armed Forces Chief Lieutenant General Fidel Ramos called a press conference and announced that they no longer supported Marcos. They called for his immediate resignation. They and the forces loyal to them had taken over Camp Aguinaldo, just outside Manila, and stood ready to defend it with tanks and automatic weapons.

When the news broke, Cory Aquino was at the home of her brother Peping, not far from the camp. Her advisers were not sure what the military revolt meant for her, and they hustled her into hiding. When asked where she thought she should stay, Cory named a nearby Carmelite monastery. The nuns welcomed her there, saying, "Cory, you will be very safe here, because they will have to kill all of us before they do anything to you." Later, Cory remarked that she slept very well, "considering that there were no mattresses."

Meanwhile, Marcos called his own press conference that evening and charged Enrile and Ramos with treason. He urged them to "stop this stupidity and surrender."

Enrile and Ramos took great pains to make it clear that they were not mounting an armed revolt. They simply wanted the rightfully elected president to take office. "I believe in my whole heart that Aquino was duly elected president," said Enrile. "She is the rightful owner of the mandate of the people."

Cory Aquino had seen some remarkable things in her life, but it was hard even for her to believe that Juan Ponce Enrile had come out in support of her. He had been a Marcos loyalist for years. He had helped Marcos impose martial law. He had held her husband in prison for seven years and seven months. He had held power over their very lives, giving or withholding permission for her to visit Ninoy or to bring others to visit him. Looking back, she realized that in some ways Enrile had been quite kind to her. After all, she had been allowed to spend every weekend with her husband. Perhaps Enrile had been having second thoughts about the excesses of the Marcos regime for a long time.

Whatever his thoughts back in the 1970s, Enrile had become seriously concerned with the state of the Philippine military in the 1980s. Under General Fabian Ver the military had become corrupt, inefficient, and unprofessional. A number of young officers were concerned about this state of affairs, and Enrile had secretly gone about organizing these men. He had hoped to bring about reforms within the military and to get General Ver out. Enrile also resented the fact that General Ver had taken over much of the power that Enrile believed belonged to him.

Lieutenant General Fidel Ramos resented Ver, too. Even though Marcos planned for Ver to retire and be replaced by Ramos, Ramos believed that Ver would continue to exercise control behind the scenes.

So the decision by Enrile and Ramos to revolt against the Marcos regime was not completely idealistic. They had personal and political motives behind their actions.

Cardinal Jaime Sin declared his support for Enrile and Ramos. Broadcasting over the church-owned Radio Veritas, he said, "Our good friends have shown their idealism. I would be very happy if you could support them now."

Marcos was furious. The next day he ordered armed combat units against Enrile, Ramos, and their supporters. But then another remarkable thing happened. Thousands of unarmed Filipinos moved in to block their way. Nuns knelt in the street and prayed. People rich and poor, young and old, wearing yellow headbands, shirts, hats, and scarves and carrying flowers stood silently side by side. As the tanks approached, they knelt down in the streets directly in the path of the oncoming armed vehicles. The tanks halted. Some soldiers left the tanks, threw down their weapons, and embraced the people in their way. Marcos might have ordered the tanks to move on, to crush the kneeling bodies in their paths. But he did not give that order. He may have been afraid that no one would obey it.

That night he appeared with his family on the government-owned TV Channel 4 and vowed to defend his government against the rebellion. But few people paid attention to him. The next day Ramos and Enrile declared a new provisional (temporary) government of the Philippines, with Cory Aquino as its head. Marcos again went on Channel 4 to call upon his supporters to come to Malacañang Palace to defend him. But suddenly his broadcast was cut off. The rebel army forces had taken over the station. Three hours later, the station's newscaster suddenly reappeared to declare: "This is the first free broadcast of Channel 4. . . . The people have taken over."

Cory watched it all with awe, but somehow the surprisingly nonviolent revolution being waged by the people did not really surprise her. She believed in miracles and in the power of flowers and prayer. She only wished that Ninoy were alive to see it.

Meanwhile, other prominent Marcos officials announced their resignations. They included the postmaster general and the customs commissioner. But Marcos continued to insist that except for a few traitors everyone in his government was loyal to him. He made plans for his inauguration the first

89

week of March. Soldiers put up barbed-wire barricades around Malacañang Palace.

Cory and her supporters, old and new, let Marcos stew in his palace while they made plans for her inauguration. This was not legal under the Marcos constitution, but her advisers believed that they had to keep building on the momentum of their movement. Juan Ponce Enrile was among those who urged her to have her own inauguration, for while Marcos might have his constitution behind him, she had the people.

On Tuesday, March 4, at the Club Filipino in the Manila suburb of Greenhills, Cory placed her left hand on a Bible and raised her right hand to take the oath of office. "I am taking power in the name of the Filipino people," she declared. "I pledge a government dedicated to upholding truth and justice, morality and decency, freedom and democracy."

It was a daylight ceremony. Cory had wanted it so. She reminded her listeners that fourteen years earlier martial law had been declared at midnight. She wanted the people to recover their rights in the full light of day.

An hour after Cory's ceremony was over, Marcos's inaugural ceremony began. He took the oath of office on the balcony of Malacañang Palace in front of four thousand cheering supporters. Then he sang several duets with his wife to entertain the invited guests in the palace ballroom. Arturo Tolentino, the man who had run for election as Marcos's vice-president, did not attend the festivities.

Cory, and even most of Marcos's supporters, did not know it, but this was the Marcoses farewell. The president had been on the telephone with the U.S. officials constantly during the previous week. While these representatives refused to advise him officially, there was no question that they considered him finished in the Philippines. About an hour after Marcos's inaugural ceremony ended, shots rang out in the

A tired and defeated Ferdinand Marcos is helped from a U.S. Air Force jet in Hawaii, where he and his family fled.

vicinity of the palace. Marcos called Enrile and demanded that he stop firing at the palace. Enrile said he had no troops there.

Then Marcos asked Enrile to call U.S. Ambassador Bosworth and ask if the United States could arrange to fly him and his family away from the palace. That same night American helicopters picked up the Marcoses, together with relatives and aides, including General Ver, and flew them to the U.S. air base. From there they were flown to Hawaii on an Air Force transport plane. Among the "personal effects" they brought along with them was over one million dollars in Philippine money.

Even the idealistic Cory found it hard to believe that it was all really happening. Three months after she had declared her candidacy, she *was* president. And Marcos was gone.

9

The First Hundred Days

There was chaos in Cory Aquino's cramped headquarters in a family-owned office building in downtown Manila. Telephones rang; people came with urgent requests to see Cory. She finally had to insist that they make appointments before they could see her. She desperately needed time to consult with her advisers, time to think. The Marcoses' leaving had come as a complete surprise. She now faced the reality of being president and of actually running the government.

First she named a Cabinet of seventeen ministers, sixteen men and one woman. She named her vice-president, Salvador Laurel, to the posts of prime minister and foreign minister, which she had promised to do in order to persuade him to run with her. She named Juan Ponce Enrile as defense minister. Since this was the post he had held under Marcos, he was the one Philippine government leader who neither lost nor gained power. She realized that these appointments would anger leftists who did not trust Laurel because he had once been a strong Marcos supporter and who were very unsure of Enrile. So she tried to balance them and other former Marcos allies with men who had long opposed Marcos. The result was a very strange political combination—people who were used to opposing each other, not working with each other. As one Philippines journalist put it, Cory's Cabinet was made up of "people you couldn't invite to a party together." Joker Arroyo, whom she named as her executive secretary and who would come to be called the "little president," had spent years accusing Enrile of human rights violations. Former Senator Jovito Salonga had been imprisoned by Enrile. Cory named Salonga to head a special Presidential Commission on Good Government. One of his duties would be to try to recover the estimated $2 billion that the Marcoses had stolen.

The Marcoses had never tried to hide their wealth, but even those who knew about it were shocked at what the couple left behind in their hasty retreat from Malacañang Palace. Most astonishing were the contents of Imelda Marcos's closets—five hundred designer gowns in silk and satin, fifteen mink coats, hundreds of bottles of perfume and jars of cosmetics, eight-hundred-eighty-eight handbags, and more than one thousand pairs of shoes! The Marcoses had a townhouse and several commercial buildings in New York that were worth an estimated $300 million. They had secret bank accounts in New York and Switzerland. As president, Marcos had earned a salary of $6,000 a year. He had stolen his wealth from the people, and Cory Aquino wanted it back.

She did not move into Malacañang Palace, although her youngest daughter, Kristina, who had spent most of her school years in the United States, wanted very much to live in a place with bathrooms that looked like those on the television program *Dallas*. Instead, Cory moved her government into a guest house on the palace grounds. She ordered that the palace itself be left just the way it was and turned into a kind of museum, a monument to excess and greed. Ordinary Filipinos could visit it and be reminded of the huge difference

President Cory Aquino with Joker Arroyo, her executive secretary. A former human rights lawyer, he came to be called the "little president."

between the way the Marcoses had lived and the way the majority of the people lived.

Some people wanted Marcos to be forced to return to the Philippines to stand trial for his crimes. In a press conference on her first full day as president, Cory hinted that she might reopen the inquiry into Ninoy's murder. But she made it clear that she would not try to force Marcos to come back to stand trial. "It is time to heal wounds and forget the past," she said.

But she also did not want him to come back because she knew there were plenty of people who still supported him. She knew that the wily old character had not given up. He would return and try to regain power at the first opportunity. As long as he was out of the country, his supporters had no one to rally around.

During her campaign, Cory had promised to release all political prisoners. Right away she ordered those who had been jailed on false charges freed. She was reluctant to release hard-line Communist insurgents and those accused of violent crimes, and she was criticized for that reluctance. Many of her followers felt that she should show as much compassion for Marcos's victims as she had for Marcos himself.

With Marcos gone, the list of victims and what they had gone through could be made public at last. Newly freed prisoners told of beatings and torture. Task Force Detainees, a Philippine religious organization that investigates detentions, reported that in 1985 alone there were 602 disappearances, 1,326 cases of torture, and 276 political executions. Cory considered naming a commission to investigate these charges.

That caused grumblings within the armed forces. Military men had been involved in these disappearances, torture, and executions. They did not want such an investigation. For her part, Cory did not want to anger the armed forces. After all, with the situation in the country as unstable as it was, and with thousands of Communist insurgents in the countryside, she could hardly disband the military. She made a few changes in the top positions, but in general she had to leave the armed forces alone, at least for the time being.

There was so much for her to do. She had inherited a struggling economy and a divided people. Many of them had united behind her and against Marcos, but already the divisions were resurfacing. It seemed to her that everyone was complaining about everything. Two days into her presidency an exasperated Cory told an audience, "Look, you people were so tolerant and patient under Marcos for twenty years, and here I am only two days and you are expecting miracles."

She was finding out, very quickly, that running against Marcos and taking his place were two entirely different things. Running against him, she could play the humble victim and get support. As president, she could no longer be humble because people wouldn't take her seriously. In fact, because she was a woman, she had to appear even more confident than a man. She worried, and she prayed, and after praying she regained her confidence. She said at the time, "My philosophy is to do everything within your capacity and then leave the rest to God. I have honestly been living that way since Ninoy's incarceration."

During her first months in office, Cory made no drastic moves, for she did not want to make any serious mistakes. She tried to address the major problems facing her and her country in small but important ways, but she wanted a thorough understanding of her options before she acted.

One gnawing problem was that technically her government was illegal. The National Assembly, the majority of whom had been Marcos men, had declared Marcos the winner of the election and had never canceled that declaration. Cory appointed a commission to study the best way to deal with the problem. In April, acting on the advice of the commission, she took a bold but necessary step.

She declared that hers was an interim government in which she would exercise not only executive powers but also the power to make laws normally enjoyed by the National Assembly. She disbanded the National Assembly and ordered the resignations of all local officials. She believed that this was the only way to root out the old Marcos regime. She promised that a new constitution would be written and that free and open elections would be held in a year.

In the remote villages and towns, the people finally began to feel the effects of Marcos's downfall. More than 80 percent of local officials had been members of Marcos's party. Many had held office for ten years or more. Cory's minister of local government, Aquilino Q. Pimentel, Jr., replaced them all with men he personally appointed. This plan drew criticism even from some of Cory's supporters, who called her a dictator just like Marcos and who pointed out that some of the local leaders had been effective. Cory answered that it was impossible to study the local leaders individually. She had to break the Marcos monopoly on local government, and this was the best way to do it.

The problem of the economy was also extremely serious. Cory appointed representatives to talk with international banks about extending the time for paying back the many loans that had been taken out by Marcos. In the middle of March she ordered a cut in fuel prices. She also asked her finance minister, Jaime Ongpin, to work with international agencies to come up with a plan for restructuring the agricultural system. As it stood, a relative few wealthy families owned all the land, and millions of farmers worked that land for little money. Cory wanted to find a way to get money

Cory learned that running against Marcos was easier than taking over his
job.   Here she explains why a new "Freedom Constitution" is necessary.

flowing out into the rural areas, where 70 percent of the people lived. She wanted the people to share in the ownership of the land they farmed. She wanted to make sure they grew enough to feed themselves and to have enough left over to sell on the world market.

Although the economic problems were among the most serious that Cory faced, she had real reason to hope for a solution. Many people around the world had been amazed at the nonviolent revolution that had overthrown Marcos and were interested in helping the Philippines solve its problems. As Jaime Ongpin put it, "We're not going to have this kind of opportunity again."

Cory also knew that she had to deal firmly and forthrightly with the Communists, whose numbers had grown as the economy had failed. By now they controlled one-fifth of the Philippines' rural areas. She had already made good on her promise to free the political prisoners, and some five hundred, including a number of Communists, had been freed. In response, Communist leaders said they would be willing to talk with her representatives. The pace of clashes between Communist rebels and government troops had slowed somewhat since Cory had taken office. But that may have been just a coincidence. Catholic nuns and priests who had gone to remote areas in unofficial attempts to arrange a cease-fire reported that some of the guerrillas did not understand that the government was now in different hands.

That was the situation with the political left. On the political right, Marcos supporters had been holding regular demonstrations against the Aquino government ever since the former president had escaped. After Aquino declared her interim government and abolished the National Assembly, they stepped up their activity. In mid-April they set up a camp across the street from the American embassy in Manila and held daily demonstrations there. Cory reminded her military troops and police that they were to show "maximum tolerance" toward the Marcos loyalists. "This is a free country now and everybody's free to say what he wants and do what he wants," she said. But she also said, "The minute they use force, the minute they resort to shooting or even to throwing stones, then I have already told the mayors to tell the police to arrest these people."

Two weeks later, on May 1, Cory addressed a labor rally, and things got out of hand. Marcos supporters chanted, "Cory! Cory! Washerwoman!" Aquino supporters answered with cries of "Marcos! Marcos! Thief!" Both sides began hurling rocks, bricks, and bottles and chasing each other through the streets. When the police tried to break up the fighting, they were hit with rocks and bottles, too.

The police tried to follow the policy of maximum tolerance and negotiated for hours with the Marcos supporters. But the negotiations failed. Eventually the police moved in with tear gas and water hoses. Thirty-three people were injured, sixty were arrested, and the encampment near the American embassy was torn down. Marcos, interviewed in Hawaii by a Manila radio station, cautioned his followers to be peaceful in their protests. But he urged them to continue and repeated that he was still president.

If Cory Aquino did not have enough to worry about, there were always those interviews with Marcos. He seemed to have a direct line to the world press, and to be using it to the fullest extent. After a period of quiet, when he admitted that he had been depressed and bitter, the former president had obviously regained his spirit and his sense of humor. He now joked that if all else failed, he could open a second-hand shoe store with his wife's one-thousand-plus pairs of shoes. He continued to pretend that he did not take Cory seriously, saying, "Poor girl, she may have bitten off more than she can chew."

As the end of her first hundred days in office approached, Cory agreed that being president was very difficult. "I am learning to say no," she admitted to *Time* magazine correspondent Sandra Burton. "I was just running myself ragged, and I wasn't myself anymore. I was just like a machine. When my first month in office was over, I got hold of myself and thought, 'This is not how it should be.' I was having such headaches. I was thinking, 'I won't last long if I keep on this way.' I am no longer so accommodating. I figure, 'I'm already president. I just don't have time.'"

To have these feelings was not at all remarkable for a new president of any country. Even those who have been in politics for years feel pressured and worried about the responsibilities of the job. What made Cory Aquino different was that she admitted to those feelings. She had not yet learned the "political game" the way veterans played it. She didn't even feel comfortable being called "President Aquino," preferring to be addressed as "President Cory" or "Mrs. President."

Still, she had done very well considering the problems she faced. In articles marking the first hundred days of her presidency in early June 1986, the world press was respectful of her. So were most Filipinos. She still enjoyed great personal popularity as a symbol of sunlight and honesty and democracy. But she had learned that to govern a troubled land one needed more than humility and generosity. It is probably no accident that by the end of the first hundred days she had started wearing dresses of other colors besides yellow. She never said so, but it is likely that she had started to realize that in politics you cannot survive on pure morality.

For most new leaders in the world, the first hundred days are easy ones, when nearly everyone is willing to give the new leader a chance to show what he or she can do. So often is this true that the first few months of office are called a "honeymoon." Cory Aquino understood the meaning of that term and didn't think it applied to her at all. "If this is a honeymoon," she said, "I'd hate to think what a nonhoneymoon would be like."

IO

Marcos Makes Trouble

Marcos supporters were working to ensure that "nonhoneymoon" for Cory Aquino. In early July, Arturo M. Tolentino, the man who had run as Marcos's vice-president in the February election, declared himself acting president on Marcos's behalf. Shortly afterward, demonstrators and armed soldiers loyal to Marcos took over the Manila Hotel. They hoped to win the backing of leaders of the armed forces. In fact, many of the soldiers later said that they thought they were being sent to support Defense Minister Juan Ponce Enrile and General Fabian Ramos. When neither Enrile nor Ramos supported them, and when civilians did not rally to their cause either, most of the soldiers surrendered. Cory ordered negotiations. The rebellion was over very soon.

One of its biggest effects was to air in public the differences between the president and her defense minister. She wanted to press charges against the rebels. Enrile wanted to grant them amnesty, or pardon. In the end, she bowed to his wishes, but she did so reluctantly. She did not like the idea that he came out of the fiasco as a savior both of the peace and of the rebel troops.

A more serious effect of the rebellion, for both the Aquino government and the Philippines, was that it caused bankers and businessmen in the rest of the world to think twice about investing in the Philippines. Nobody wanted to invest in an unstable country where there were serious questions about the army's loyalty to the government. Cory had been counting on those investors to help the Philippine economy.

In August, the government got some money from the Marcoses, though it was involuntary financial help. The contents of the Marcos townhouse in New York were auctioned off. It was estimated that Imelda Marcos had spent $100 million for jewelry, art, and furniture in New York in the past ten years. The auction brought only a fraction of that amount. Still, the auction was a reminder of how much the Marcoses had stolen.

And later that month, there was a reminder of how many lives Marcos had ruined. Cory Aquino dedicated a shrine to her late husband. It was a flat granite slab embedded in the runway of Manila Airport, and it was etched with the figure of a man in the very same position as Ninoy Aquino had been after he had fallen, dead, from the steps of the Taiwan airliner. When police investigate the scene of a murder, they make an outline of the murdered victim's body with chalk before they move the body. This etched figure was like a permanent outline of the body of the murdered hero.

Cory wanted to be alone that day. The public statements were made by her ministers. Said her minister of agrarian reform, Heherson Alvarez, "We showed the world that Ninoy did not die in vain. Now we must wage war against ourselves, against our own indiscipline and apathy. It is no longer as clear and simple as a war against a dictator."

Two weeks later, President Corazon Aquino made her first trip outside the Philippines since she had come to power. She visited neighboring Indonesia, explaining, "There has not been any doubt that my first visit abroad as president should be to our neighbors." She left at a time of unrest, but she had concluded that unrest was going to be something she would have to live with. Some of her advisers warned that dissidents in the military might try to take over the government in her absence. She stated that she could trust her cabinet and military officers, and added, just in case, that she was sure the Filipino people would help "anytime there is need to protect the peace of our country."

There were no crises while President Cory was away. But almost as soon as she returned she faced a serious one. Her defense minister, Juan Ponce Enrile, was becoming more and more open in his criticism of her dealings with the Communist rebels. He was absolutely against her attempts to make peace with them. He also did not like her talking peace with Moslem rebels in Mindanao. But he was most concerned about the Communist insurgents. Over the past few months, he had argued more and more strongly in Cabinet meetings against any sort of truce with the Communists. Now he was beginning to criticize her publicly. He was supposed to accompany her on her first visit to the United States as president in September. He decided to remain in the Philippines, saying he wanted to stay behind to prove that he would not try to overthrow her government in her absence.

Cory considered her visit to the United States very important. She hoped to persuade the U.S. Congress to grant the Philippines more aid. During her nine-day visit she went to Boston, New York, and San Francisco, as well as to Washington, D.C. She impressed many people in the United States during her visit. The Speaker of the House of Representatives, Thomas P. O'Neill, said that the speech she gave before Congress was the best one he had heard in his thirty-four years in Congress.

The Congress proved to be a friendly audience. In her honor the lawmakers wore yellow shirts, blouses, sweaters, neckties, or flowers in their lapels. They interrupted her speech eleven times with applause. In her speech, she stressed her belief that she had to do whatever she could to make peace with the Communists. She said, "My predecessor set aside democracy to save it from a Communist insurgency that numbered less than five hundred. Unhampered by respect for human rights, he went at it with hammer and tongs. By the time he fled, that insurgency had grown to more than sixteen thousand. I think there is a lesson here to be learned about trying to stifle a thing with the means by which it grows. . . . As president, I will not betray the cause of peace by which I came to power. Yet equally, and again no friend of Filipino democracy will challenge this, I will not stand by and allow an insurgent leadership to spurn our offer of peace and kill our young soldiers and threaten our new freedom. Yet I must explore the path of peace to the utmost, for at its end, whatever disappointment I meet there, is the moral basis for laying down the olive branch of peace and taking up the sword of war."

The House of Representatives voted to increase aid to the Philippines. But the Senate voted against such an increase. Cory was deeply disappointed, for she had been counting on that additional aid to help solve some of the terrible problems of the Philippine economy.

Still, her trip to the United States was successful in terms of public relations. She showed that she could be a very capable stateswoman and that she could combine her deep faith with a sense of hard political reality.

President Aquino shakes hands with Speaker of the U.S. House of Representatives, Thomas P. O'Neill, Jr. O'Neill said that the speech she gave before Congress was the best he'd heard in his 34 years there.

During her trip to the United States, Cory enjoyed a reunion with her former classmates at the College of Mount St. Vincent.

During her visit to Washington, D.C., she went to church at the National Shrine of the Immaculate Conception. An audience of two thousand Filipinos and Americans heard her explain that prayers are answered "in unforeseen ways" and that the answers are not always easy for humans to understand. "I do not always understand why it is I who am president of a free country today, except that I, who was not made for politics, became involved in politics and helped lead the revolution that deposed Mr. Marcos last February." She asked, "Why did a dictator open his mouth on American television and call a snap election? And who stayed the hand of Marcos as his forces poised to smash us?" Her faith intact, Cory Aquino returned to the Philippines.

Shortly after her return, the army arrested a top Communist leader named Rodolfo Salas as he left a Manila hospital after a medical checkup. Immediately, other rebel leaders warned that peace talks between the Communists and the government could not continue while Salas was in custody. Some supporters of President Aquino wondered about the timing of the arrest, suspecting that it was a deliberate attempt by the army to undermine the peace talks. But Joker Arroyo insisted that it was just a coincidence. Salas was charged with "war against the forces of government, destroying property and committing serious violence." Cory directed that peace talks with the Communists continue.

In late October, the commission she had appointed to draft a new constitution presented its document to Cory, who quickly approved it. Most of the document was very democratic, establishing a two-house legislature and a system of checks and balances similar to that outlined in the U.S. Constitution. Like the 1943 constitution, it called for a president to serve a single term of six years and to be democratically elected by the people. The big difference was that it contained a "transitory provision" that endorsed a six-year term for Cory, until June 30, 1992.

What this provision meant was that Cory's government would be given the legal basis it had abandoned in March when she, as president, had abolished the 1973 charter under which she had been elected. Since doing away with that charter, she had headed what she called a revolutionary government under a temporary "freedom constitution." Without this "transitory provision" in the new constitution, her government was not actually legal.

Many people were unhappy with that provision, which applied only to President Corazon Aquino. They believed that if the new constitution was approved by the Filipino people, Cory Aquino should stand for reelection. Only if she won election as president under the new constitution would her presidency be legal. Among them was Juan Ponce Enrile. He believed that Cory should submit to new presidential elections. He argued that she had lost her mandate to govern when she abandoned the 1973 Marcos constitution, under which the last elections had been held.

Enrile was becoming more and more outspoken. He was now saying that it was the military that had "handed power" to her. Salvador Laurel, Cory's vice-president, seemed to agree with Enrile. He proposed a nationwide vote of confidence in the Aquino government. At the regular Cabinet meeting in the last week of October, Enrile refused to sit next to Cory, and Laurel stayed away, saying he had a cold. Two days later, General Fidel Ramos made public statements against the Communists. He seemed to be siding with Enrile as well.

For several weeks, Enrile had been addressing anti-Communist rallies. But in one such rally in the last week of October, he not only attacked Cory but seemed to align himself

111

with the supporters of Marcos when he charged that her government was corrupt. At this point, Cory's supporters decided that Enrile had gone too far. They urged her to take action against him. Cory hesitated. She explained that she had to be really convinced that Enrile was doing something deliberate to destabilize her government.

During the first week of November, Cory announced the schedule for making her government legal. On February 2, 1987, the nation would vote on the new constitution. This would put the government on a firm legal basis. Then, on May 11, 1987, there would be elections to the new national legislature. There would be no special presidential election. When asked about this, she explained, "No, when the people voted in the February 7 [1986] election, they knew it was for a term of six years. They did not think the term was just for a while. That's very, very clear." After the six years were up, would she run again? No, she did not intend to seek reelection as president in 1992. By that time, she hoped to be able to hand over the office to a new, democratically elected president.

Two days later, General Ramos was reporting that he had uncovered a plan by some military officers to overthrow the "inept and left-leaning" members of the government but to retain Cory as president. The plan may have been hatched in response to real progress in the government's talks with the Communists. There was no question that rightists were willing to do anything to keep a truce from being declared.

In fact, in the second week of November, Rolando Olalia, one of the major leftist leaders, head of the nation's largest labor union, was killed. The hope may have been to create a leftist backlash, which in turn would justify a military crackdown. But no such backlash occurred. Cory vowed to

Armed Forces Chief General Fidel Ramos assures the press that the military are strongly behind President Aquino.

investigate the murder, and the leftists kept on talking about the terms of a truce.

In the third week of November, yet another plan by some military officers to overthrow the government was uncovered. This time, Defense Minister Juan Ponce Enrile was clearly involved. General Ramos, who had led the rebellion of the previous February with Enrile, uncovered the plot and sided with Cory. Finally Cory had to act. In an emergency meeting, she asked for the resignations of all seven members of her Cabinet. She accepted that of Enrile. She then gave the Communist insurgents seven days to agree to a cease-fire.

Many in her government, not to mention her supporters outside the government, were relieved that she had taken a strong stand at last. They had worried that she seemed indecisive and weak. That was no longer the case. She had come out strongly and made the hard decisions that were necessary. "It has often been said that Marcos was the first male chauvinist to underestimate me," she told a women's group a couple of days later. "He was not the last to pay for that mistake." Referring to Marcos's remark during the campaign that a woman's place is in the bedroom, she said, "It is not I who have been consigned to the bedroom of history."

At the end of the seven-day deadline, the Communist leaders formally agreed to a sixty-day cease-fire. It could not have come at a better time. It would extend to just past the February 2 vote on the new constitution, approval of which would build the strength of her government.

II

Legal President at Last

Cory had finally succeeded in making good on her campaign promise to make peace with the Communists, at least for a time. There were many other promises on which she had not yet made good, and she knew that. The Philippines was in such a mess when she took over that she simply could not solve all the problems in the space of a single year. She had decided that the most important thing was to have a cease-fire so that all sectors of the population could work together in an atmosphere of peace in order to make their lives better.

The next important thing was to give her government a legal basis and to lay the foundation for a democratic government with a two-chamber legislature. The new constitution would do that, and in early January 1987 Cory began to campaign for its passage.

In many ways, this campaign was like a second presidential campaign. The continuation of her presidency rested on the people's acceptance of the new constitution (in its "transitory provision" making her president until June 30, 1992).

So did the democratic policies that she had put in place during the months she had led the government. She believed that a good-sized majority of the people must vote in favor of the new constitution if she were to be able to govern effectively. One of her spokesmen, Teodoro Benigno, said that they would not consider as a victory anything less than a 65 percent vote in favor of the new constitution.

Cory traveled all around the Philippines to ask for the people's support. She also announced the creation of a new job program, which would take effect just before the vote on the constitution. Opponents charged that Cory was trying to bribe the people, just as Marcos had done. Yes, Cory's supporters admitted privately, this was "patronage politics" but of a more "enlightened" kind. Why was it more enlightened? Said one economic adviser, "It's more enlightened because they don't like to do it." In other words, the Cory government hoped that the people would vote for the new constitution because it was a good, democratic document. But they believed in its importance and understood that the poor people were more interested in jobs than freedom. So they were willing to play the "political game" in some ways to see that it was passed.

But mostly Cory appealed to the people in the same way as she had done when she was campaigning for the presidency. "I know you still love me," she told a cheering crowd in Legaspi. She spoke of democracy and freedom. She spoke of the death of Ninoy. She asked that the people "please be patient" and promised that she would help get them out of their poverty.

Meanwhile, the opposition had mounted its own campaign to defeat the new constitution. This opposition included people on both the left and the right.

Signs like this one urged Filipino people to vote for the new constitution.

Some had real grievances. On January 22, ten thousand people, many of them farmers demanding a change in land-ownership policies, demonstrated outside Malacañang Palace. They pushed against the lines of police and military troops that surrounded the palace. The front-line troops held out shields that were stenciled in yellow with the words "Maximum Tolerance." These were the words for Cory's policy of allowing free people to demonstrate in a free nation. But when shots came from the ranks of the demonstrators, the police and military responded by opening fire. There was instant chaos, and still more shots from the military and police. When it was over, twelve protesters were dead, and Cory's government was in trouble.

Opponents on the right charged that the protest showed that she was weak and incompetent. Opponents on the left charged that her government would not allow protest. Cory called an emergency meeting and ordered an investigation into what happened. She also went on national television to say, "In the period before the [vote on the constitution], attempts to destabilize the government will intensify. We are prepared for this contingency. We shall have order throughout our land."

It was a tense time for Cory, but in the midst of the tension there was new hope. Immediately after the incident at the palace, a group of Western nations that had lent money to the Philippines agreed to easier repayment terms. It was very clearly a show of support for Cory and her government.

Cory needed all the support she could get, for in the Philippines she was being criticized from all sides. On the left, Communist negotiators suspended peace talks with the government, saying that their lives had been threatened. Leaders of the farmer's march announced that they would hold another march. This time Cory did not send troops to protect the palace. In fact, she sent her Cabinet ministers and secretaries, who were joined by other Cory supporters. There was no violence.

Here is how an editorial in *The New York Times* described the situation: "How Corazon Aquino must enrage her foes: she refuses to fight like a man. On the left, zealots thirst for martyrs and shootings, the stuff of revolution. So what does the president of the Philippines do? She opens her palace to fist-shaking demonstrators and orders her Cabinet ministers to greet them, for heaven's sake, in an arms-linked human chain of bureaucrats, businessmen, students, and Roman Catholic nuns.

"One can hear revolutionaries fuming at this stratagem, so obviously calculated to win votes in next Monday's [vote] on the new constitution framed by Mrs. Aquino's year-old government. One can hear the right-wing reactionaries as well, bemoaning their adversaries' failure to produce chaos."

The right-wing reactionaries did not sit around moaning for long. On January 27 a group of army rebels attempted to take over key military camps, broadcasting stations, and public utilities. They were successful only in taking over a private television and radio station. Once again, General Fidel Ramos had learned of the plot and used loyal troops to beat back the rebels. After holding out at the TV and radio station for a time, the rebels there finally surrendered.

That very day, January 29, the news came out that this was not just an isolated uprising on the part of a few army rebels. This was part of a major offensive that would bring Ferdinand Marcos back into power in the Philippines. In fact, if it had not been for actions on the part of the United States, Marcos would have been back in the Philippines already.

Over in Honolulu, Hawaii, Tomas Gomez, the Philippine consul in Hawaii, became suspicious about a chartered Boeing

707 airplane that had arrived from Miami and just sat at the Honolulu airport as if waiting for something. He informed the Philippine embassy in Washington, D.C., which in turn alerted the U.S. State Department.

The State Department learned that the plane had been chartered by Marcos supporters. The only possible reason was a plan to fly Marcos to the Philippines. Meanwhile, Imelda Marcos went on an unusual shopping trip. At the Military Shop in Waikiki, she and several other people spent $2,000 in cash on camouflage pants, combat boots, T-shirts, and flight jackets.

After conferences with Cory's representatives, U.S. representatives went to see Marcos and told him that he would not be allowed to leave Honolulu. When the United States had agreed to give Marcos safe passage to Honolulu, Marcos had agreed not to return to the Philippines without the permission of the Philippine government. He also agreed to notify the United States of any plans to leave Honolulu for any destination. The United States told him he had to keep that agreement. Said Marcos, "Now I am being treated like a prisoner."

A couple of days later, Marcos announced that an eye ailment prevented him from flying. This may have been his way of encouraging his supporters not to give up hope (that he would be able to come back once his eye was better). Or it may have been a way to save face (he was embarrassed that he had been outwitted by the U.S. government). What was clear was that there would be no Marcos return before the vote on the new constitution.

Back in the Philippines, President Aquino took her strongest steps yet against pro-Marcos forces in the military. She ordered that the rebels involved in the takeover of the TV station be court-martialed, or made to stand trial in military courts. This was a far cry from the punishment of thirty pushups that the rebels had gotten away with the previous July.

She also made strong statements about her policy toward the Communist insurgents. The peace talks had broken down, and Cory made it clear that if the leaders of the Communists refused to negotiate, she was willing to take other steps. She knew that she had tried the peaceful route and now had a firm moral basis for "taking up the sword."

On February 2, the day of the vote on the new constitution, the atmosphere at the crowded polling places was remarkably peaceful. While the military was on the alert against possible violence, there were few reports of trouble. The evening before, there had been three small explosions in Manila, but no one had been injured. In general, the opposition to Cory and the constitution, on both the right and the left, seemed to have collapsed.

There was almost a holiday atmosphere at many polling places. The people seemed to feel good about voting and to feel safe voting for the first time in many, many years. The sunlight that Cory had promised to bring to the Philippines was bright on that day, and when all the votes were counted, the new constitution had been approved by a landslide.

Cory knew that there were many problems ahead. She still hadn't gotten the Communist rebels under control. She didn't even have her own military under control. And as long as Ferdinand Marcos was alive, she knew she faced attempts to overthrow her government and reinstate his. Her country still faced serious economic problems, and she realized she had to deal forcefully with them. The most difficult problem was land reform. She had not made good on her promises for real change in who owned the land and benefited from the crops that were produced on it. She herself was from a wealthy, landowning family. So were most of the members of

An elderly Filipino checks the voting rolls at a polling station.

Ballot boxes containing votes on the new constitution are turned in to election commission employees.

her Cabinet and most of the people she hoped would be elected to the legislature in May. Some people wondered if her government was capable of real land reform.

But now, at least she had a firm legal basis to work from in trying to solve those problems. She knew that she had only until June 1992 to bring about the changes she wanted in the Philippines. But she believed that with the people behind her she could accomplish what she had set out to do. And now there was no question that the people were behind her. She knew it, Marcos knew it, the Communists knew it, the world knew it. And she hoped that somehow Ninoy knew it, too.

Index

124

About the Author

James Haskins is a teacher, lecturer, and widely published author. He is a recipient of the Coretta Scott King award for *The Story of Stevie Wonder.*

Mr. Haskins traveled to the Philippines in 1980 when he was editing the three-volume encyclopedia, *Our Filipino Nation.* He came away with a strong sense that the Filipino people have their own identity and their own soul and the strength to forge their own destiny. He believes that President Corazon C. Aquino has the capacity to lead her people to that destiny.

James Haskins is the author of a number of books published by Enslow Publishers, including *Leaders of the Middle East* and *About Michael Jackson.*